MORE
HEALEYS

MORE HEALEYS

Frog-eyes, Sprites
and Midgets

GEOFFREY HEALEY

GENTRY BOOKS
LONDON

Published by Gentry Books Limited,
16 Regency Street, London SW1.
Distributed in the USA by

Osceola, Wisconsin 54020, USA

Filmset by Computer Photoset, Limited, Birmingham.
Printed and bound in Great Britain by
William Clowes & Sons Limited,
London, Beccles and Colchester.

Contents

Acknowledgments

The author gratefully acknowledges the following for their kind permission to reproduce photographs: *Autocar*, *Motor*, British Leyland, Alan Burman, Edward Eves, Kevin Faughnan, Brian Foley, Newswest/International, R. Petalowski, Daniel Rubin, Alan Zafer, John Wright Photography.

He would like to point out that it has not been possible to trace the source of all the photographs and wishes to apologise to anyone who is not included in this list for this reason.

Foreword

I am delighted to write the foreword to Geoff's new book about Sprites and Midgets, as this will do much to balance the Austin Healey story. The Big Healey was always given the greater share of publicity but it was the Sprite that introduced so many thousands to the fun of sports car motoring. Once they had sampled sports cars they rarely or only briefly returned to a mass production saloon. So many people had bemoaned the passing of the small MG Midgets and Austin Seven sports cars of the thirties that it was a logical move to bring back a car that filled this gap.

I feel that the decline in our motor industry stems from the time when the motormen lost control and were replaced by people with little understanding of the industry, not having the love for a motorcar that is fundamental to producing a winner. I am amazed that our rulers give vast sums of aid to foreign motorcar manufacturers when if only a very small portion of this aid was given to our British firms we would have many more British cars—not to mention a much healthier balance of payments.

Geoff does not take enough credit for his own achievements and efforts in creating sports cars. In the past, he always toed the BMC publicity line which was built around me. This may have given rise to the myth that Geoff had little ability at drawing, but if he had not drawn so much and so well there certainly would not have been so many Austin Healeys on the roads today. I am glad that Geoff now appears more in the public view at Club Meets and that he has become more outspoken.

I am sure that this book will redress the balance and provide a source of useful information to many Sprite and Midget owners.

Happy Healeying,

Donald Healey

Introduction

When I wrote my first book, *Austin Healey : The Story of the Big Healeys* I thought that that was all anyone would want to know about Austin Healeys. The reception it got exceeded the wildest hopes of all concerned. My phone rang more often since its publication than it ever did during the most active days with the Austin Healey – and what a different type of call! Instead of the usual grumble about lack of performance or drivers who had lost their way between Abingdon and Warwick, there were enthusiasts complimenting me on the book.

However, for every ten who were very happy, there would be twenty who wanted more and particularly more about Sprites. Now Sprite owners have often felt like the poor relations in the past. A Sprite was only half the price of the Big Healey and Sprite owners were not always given the welcome and respect they deserved at the factory. They were more numerous and generally did not have the same amount of money to spend. What some people forgot was that Sprite owners probably got more enjoyment out of their cars than the big boys. One piece of good to come out of the first book has been the closer co-operation that now exists between the two camps.

Nowadays people have discovered my hideaway and many an old friend has called to discuss the book and those happy days. Geoff Cooper and his encyclo-paedic memory helped me to put a few more pieces of the jigsaw together. I have never met anybody who could recall technical and design details so accurately. In the old days, Geoff always knew which parts would fit together from the various models, and which were the best to use. People like him are rare in the industry today.

British Leyland have now formed a museum and are rather belatedly building up a collection. Unfortunately, new brooms often sweep clean, and during the various reorganizations much valuable material has been lost. However, members of the Healey family have always tended to hoard. We never believed in destroying the old, but kept it so that we should not make the same mistake twice! The reaction of many of my relatives and friends has been that here was a way in which this cherished material could at last be put to good use. I thought I had a lot when I started my first book, but now the house bulges with history. The insurance company has even insisted on more locks and larger premiums, as so much of it is irreplaceable.

My mother received the first book with unusual rapture and, being in the mood, gave me the remains of her photograph albums. DMH unearthed a vast quantity of photographs and film. He has always been something of a photographer and invariably took a camera with him when racing. My brother Brian was also inspired to go through his scrap books of cuttings and photographs and came up with a lot of useful Sprite material.

I have been very fortunate in being concerned with the Austin Healeys longer than almost anyone else, from those nights when under my father's guidance I laid down the first lines on paper in the attic of our house in Leamington Spa. I was always taught to record details on paper and to keep my notes and drawing for reference purposes. This has left me with several thousand drawings, many superb works of draughtsmanship by experts such as Len Hodges, Barry Bilbie and Gerry Coker.

I am also fortunate in that Margot, my long suffering wife, is an excellent typist and is able to decipher and type my scribbled writing at no cost to me. (Little does he know! Typist's note.) Again, my publisher Lorna Gentry has been able to guide me in explaining details that are clear to me but would be obscure to so many readers.

I am continually being asked to name my favourite car, usually in the form of a leading question, such as 'The 100S was the best, wasn't it?' Over the twenty-six years covering the life of the Austin Healey, I was able to drive all the models—the good, the bad and the indifferent. One's preference naturally changes with time, as something new and better is developed. Of the pre-Austin-era cars, the 2.4 litre Roadster with which I competed in two Mille Miglia races stands out. It was better than the standard production cars in that Roger Menadue built it with such care. It would do 112 mph on the level but I would not endure those grabbing, locking, fading, rumbling brakes for long. When I last tried one, I realized that we had made some progress. Silverstones were fun, too, with more forgiving handling but fewer creature comforts.

The first Healey Hundred was a real step forward in every way, though one missed the central remote control of the old Riley gearbox. Then came the production Austin Healey and the Special Test cars. The one I used in 1953 was enormous fun—fast, reliable and economical. The Laycock overdrive unit in competition form was a wonderful feature, giving no less than seven beautifully spaced speeds, so that one always had the right gear at the right moment. The 100S coupé was a great step forward in performance, braking and handling, and is remembered with affection. Snug in the winter, it was a bit like a hothouse in the summer, despite all our efforts to improve the ventilation. Until the 6 cylinder was opened out to 3 litres it offered little improvement other than a smoother-running engine. With development, the brakes, suspension, gearbox and power unit were improved to make the 3000 a most civilized and potent machine. Again, I loved the Warwick-built competition cars with their light-weight bodies, near 200 bhp and excellent handling.

But of all the cars, I think that the one I enjoyed driving the most was the special Sprite we built for the 1965 Targa Florio. It was fast with a top speed of 125 mph, it was economical, giving 35 mpg on the road, it was comfortable and its handling was precise. It leaked water but that was about its only vice. Many who drove this car considered it to be one of the best handling conventional sports cars of all time. I still have the drawings which I keep in the hope of making another one!

I have always been used to engineering, where fact and accuracy is the most important consideration and I have attempted to record the story of the Sprite and the Midget without hiding too many of our mistakes. If you make and create much, you must make some mistakes.

Donald Healey and his Early Cars

Donald Mitchell Healey–DMH–joined the motor trade in 1918, at the age of twenty. His early training was in aviation–he had been apprenticed to the Sopwith Aviation Company and served as a Royal Flying Corps pilot during the 1914–18 war. However, when he returned home to Perranporth, Cornwall, war service had somewhat dampened his enthusiasm for aircraft.

His father bought the piece of waste land next to his shop, the Red House at Perranporth, and on it erected the Red House Garage. DMH did not find running a garage enough to occupy him and took to competition motoring. He competed in the Truro Motor Club's local events with various cars, including the overhead valve Buick, and developed the taste for motor sport. In those days this meant reliability trials, of which pride of place went to the Motor Cycling Club's London-Land's End Trial at Easter. Starting outside London, the motorcycles, three-wheelers and cars would set forth at intervals for the hills of the West Country–Porlock Hill in Somerset, Beggars Roost in Devon and Blue Hills Mine just outside Perranporth, with a final run down to Land's End. These hills and the run were a test for the cars of the day whereas now even a Japanese car could deal with them.

Preparing his cars at Perranporth, DMH won gold medals in rallies with ABC, Ariel, Rover, Fiat and Triumph. None of these cars could be described as sporting, apart, perhaps, from the supercharged Triumph Seven with which he won the 1929 Brighton Rally. He next turned to foreign events. He finished seventh in the 1930 Monte Carlo Rally with a Triumph Seven

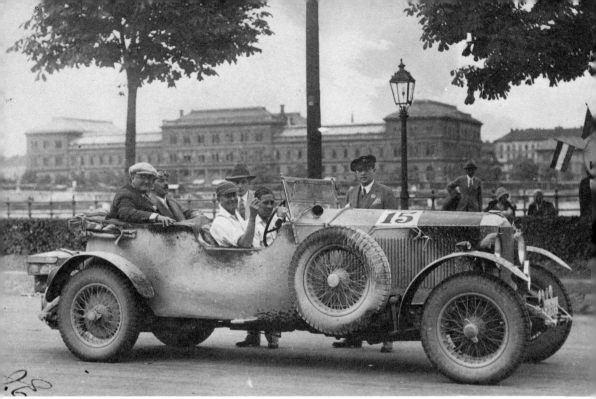

The 1930 Austrian Alpine Trial, won by DMH on the 4½ litre Invicta—naturally equipped with Dunlop tyres, Lucas electrics and SU carburettors.

and was then given his first real works drive with a real car by Captain Macklin. With the 4½ litre Invicta, DMH, Vic Horsmann, G. H. Rayner and a 17½ stone Austrian journalist, Professor Wolfbauer, won an Alpine Cup in the 1930 Austrian Alpine Trial, repeating their success in the Austro-Hungarian Alpine Trial shortly afterwards. This Invicta was not the then new low chassis 100 mph model but an older model with which a team of lady drivers had won the Dewar Trophy in 1929 for doing 30,000 miles in 30,000 minutes. DMH always maintained that the older car handled better than the later one. It certainly did not spin out of control so suddenly. The big low revving Meadows engines ensured good performance in these comparatively light cars.

For the 1931 Monte Carlo Rally DMH prepared the newer low chassis Invicta at Perranporth and with Vic Horsman and fellow Cornishman Lewis Pearce won the Rally outright. His friend Vic Leverett won the small car class with a Riley. The following year DMH finished in second place, again with the trusty Invicta.

In 1933 DMH joined the Riley experimental department and moved to lodgings with the Thompson family in Barford, near Warwick, next door to what is now the Joseph Arch public house. The current Riley engines were a development of the traditional Riley design. Two camshafts high in the cylinder block operated the overhead valves in a hemispherical cylinder head. With its good breathing, this design ensured excellent power and DMH

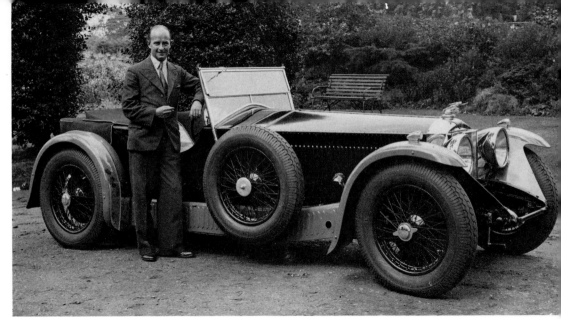

DMH with one of the low chassis Invictas with which he won the 1931 Monte Carlo Rally. The device on the radiator cap is a replica of a trophy awarded each year to the first driver to finish within the first three places in three events. DMH won this trophy outright in 1934.

The low chassis 4½ litre Invicta prepared for the Monte Carlo Rally, under test at Perranporth.

The 1934 Monte Carlo Rally. The two Triumph Gloria cars display their large section tyres. The scoop at the base of windscreen was an early defroster. Similar front mud flaps are often used on rally cars today. (Motor)

DMH adjusting carburettors on the Climax-engined Triumph during the 1934 Alpine Rally.

competed successfully in many rallies with various Riley models.

The following year, he joined Triumph, first as experimental manager, and later becoming technical director. With Tommy Wisdom, he took a Triumph to third place in the 1934 Monte Carlo Rally, starting from Athens. One feature on this car was its Dunlop 9.00 × 16 tyres: the use of wide tyres on sports cars was not to return until thirty years later. Seven Triumphs entered this event, all fitted with Coventry Climax engines of 1232 cc with overhead inlet valves and side exhaust valves, and all seven cars finished the course.

DMH was responsible for the Gloria and Dolomite series of Triumph cars. The most interesting design was the straight eight Triumph Dolomite of 2 litres' capacity, based on the 2.3 litre Alfa Romeo. Under an arrangement between the two companies, Triumph supplied details of the Triumph motor cycle which Alfa Romeo considered manufacturing in Italy while Triumph produced the Dolomite in England. The bore of the engine was reduced in order to reduce the amount of road tax paid under the old system, whereby tax was assessed under the so-called RAC rating. This horsepower rating system favoured the use of long stroke engines and was responsible for hamstringing many designs in Britain. For a 2 litre supercharged engine, the power output was disappointing. The bore size was later enlarged to give 2.3 litres' capacity, resulting in a greatly improved performance. The body styling of the Triumph

Lewis Pearce, DMH's co-driver, with the Triumph Dolomite before the start of 1935 Monte Carlo Rally. The car is equipped with hooded Lucas fog lights and an extra sidemounted fuel tank.

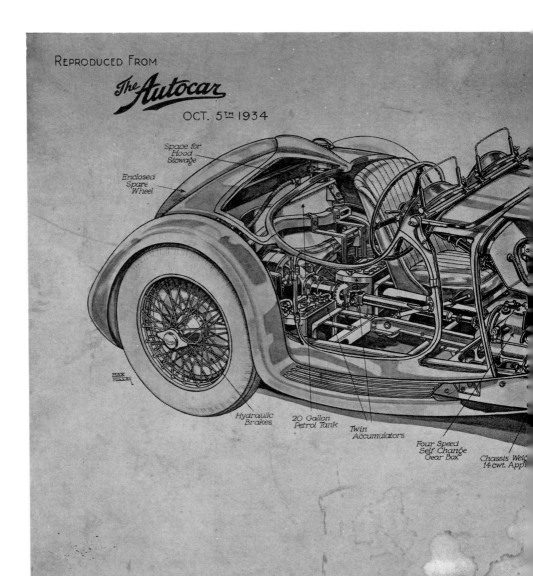

The Autocar

OCT. 5TH 1934

Space for Hood Stowage

Enclosed Spare Wheel

MAX MILLAR

Hydraulic Brakes

20 Gallon Petrol Tank

Twin Accumulators

Four Speed Self Change Gear Box

Chassis Weig 14 cwt. Appr

" TRIUMPH

Max Millar, one of the greatest artists of all time, produced this splendid drawing for The Autocar (now Autocar). This high standard of artistic presentation continues to the present day. Triumph revived the Dolomite name for their popular small car range.

Twin Overhead
Camshafts

Central
Camshaft
Drives

2 Litre
"Straight Eight"
Engine
60 × 88 m.m. Bore & Stroke
1990cc.
R.A.C. Rating 18 H.P.

Supercharger

Air Intake

3 Gallon
Oil Reservoir

DOLOMITE"

cars was the responsibility of Walter Bellgrove. He was later to design the TR2 which was to provide the main opposition to the Austin Healey.

Triumph should have been in for a period of stability and growth with their new cars. Harry Weslake, one of Britain's master tuners, had been called in to improve the engine performance and as always produced the goods. Triumph used to buy the gears for the gearboxes from Austin but under the confident assertion of their new works manager that they could do better, they started to make them at Coventry. The resulting Triumph-produced gears were disastrous and it was not until Harry Brandish was given a free hand that this change bore success. Even so, the decision of the bank to call in a receiver came as a complete surprise to everyone. There seemed to be no logical reason for the move. Triumph were well placed with an excellent range of cars, their bank overdraft was well below the agreed limit, and the war then looming up would put a premium on factory capacity. However, what can best be described as a fit of pique on the part of the bank's representative caused the end of the company.

During the war DMH ran the Triumph factory for the Ministry of Aircraft Production, producing Hobson aircraft carburettors and controls. He later moved to Humber to work on armoured fighting vehicles. Here he formed the association with A. C. (Sammy) Sampietro and B. G. (Ben) Bowden that was to result in his forming the Donald Healey Motor Company and the subsequent birth of the Healey cars.

EYF 375 – one of the original MG Midgets. DMH owned this during the war. Cecil Kimber of MG gave him a short stroke engine and DMH fitted 16 inch wheels with wider tyres which improved the road holding.

The first Healey chassis inside Benford's factory at Warwick. It is being equipped with a minimum of fittings to enable it to be tested. It was known as the 'Horror' amongst friends.

Sammy Sampietro, DMH, Ben Bowden and the first Healey car at Honiley. The RAF station at Honiley is now a Girling test ground. We aimed to have flaps that opened over headlamps but this feature was not developed to save costs. The registration number is a phoney one.

The competition involvement of motor companies had a direct effect on their products. Those involved – Bentley, Triumph, Riley, MG, Invicta, Alfa Romeo, Jaguar and so on – produced exciting cars. Those not involved just produced reliable but dull transport vehicles. The prime objective of competition was obtaining publicity to improve sales and much that was new stemmed from competition development. Competition also expanded the knowledge of those concerned and most of the best engineers and designers were involved – men like Harry Weslake, Walter Hassan, Harry Mundy, Sydney Enever, Eddie Maher, Spen King, Peter Wilks, Charles Griffin, Alec Issigonis, Geoff Johnson, Colin Chapman, Peter Wilson, Alan Zafer, Stuart Turner, Arkus Duntov . . .

The design and development of the first two Healey models, the 2.4 litre Saloon and Roadster, commonly referred to as the Elliot and the Westland after the body builders, has been described in my first book, *Austin Healey: The Story of the Big Healeys*. Although these models had the greatest competition success, the Healey Silverstone has since become the most sought after and valuable of these early Healey cars. The original design for this was based on the standard 2.4 litre chassis and one prototype was built, known as the 'Red Bug'. This car was nose heavy, due to the forward position of the engine, which also made it ugly. Its body was constructed by Cape Engineering, a then small company located a short distance from the Healey factory at the Cape. This company was set up by an old friend of ours from the motor industry, Gerry Turner, and was primarily concerned with light alloy construction work for the aircraft and defence industries. Under Gerry, Cape Engineering has since grown to be a large and prosperous organization.

The 'Red Bug' incorporated air suspension at the rear. These units were invented by Peter Thornhill and produced by Automotive Products of Leamington Spa. Similar in appearance to direct acting or telescopic dampers, they were very much a new concept, with little in the way of road development behind them. The Sampietro-designed Healey suspension had always been in trouble at the rear. Wheel movement was too limited and the space available for the springs resulted in their being overstressed. Despite the efforts of the best spring makers of the day, Tempered Springs of Sheffield and their Mr Fryer, spring failure was all too frequent. Small firms do not have the funds or manpower to carry out extensive development and so the possibility that the Thornhill air springs might offer a solution to our problems had to be put to the test. In fact, they were not that successful on the 'Red Bug', tending to heat up and give an increase in ride height after a short time.

Len Hodges, our designer, was now given a free hand to design an improved car. Len was a very competent draughtsman and a very fine engineer. He was also responsible for creating the system and standard of engineering within the organization that were to stand us in good stead throughout later develop-

X1: the Red Bug, in Italy with Achille (Sammy) Sampietro and DMH for Alpine tests in 1947. This was the first attempt at a low cost sports car that led to the creation of the Silverstone. Note the Dunlop centre lock wire wheels.

ments. Like many other engineers, Len tended to be somewhat absent-minded when it came to non-engineering matters. A tale he told us one Monday morning illustrated this. He had had to go to Woolworths on Saturday to buy some curtain hooks for the house. Armed with instructions he set forth in his 1930 Austin Seven saloon and parked it at the back of Woolworths. Having obtained the appropriate hooks, he then left by the front door and climbed onto a push bike which he rode home. On going to put the bike away in the hall he found another similar bike in its place. This caused Len to scratch his head until what had happened finally dawned on him. He quickly rode back to Woolworths, parked the bike and retrieved his Austin Seven. Absent minded as he was about mundane matters, he was concise and meticulous with the work of the drawing office. He insisted on an extremely high standard and simple parts drawn under his instructions were works of art.

On the Silverstone design, Len decided to incorporate some telescopic dampers made by Newton and Bennett. These dampers were at that time the best available and did much to improve the handling of the car. Instead of

The prototype Silverstone under construction at the Cape Works, Warwick.

shortening the chassis wheelbase the engine was repositioned 6 inches further aft. The car was designed to be produced and sold at under £1000, thereby avoiding the doubling of purchase tax. The Government in its wisdom or in pursuit of taxing the rich had decided that cars costing more than £1000 were to be subject to twice the tax. This penalty had to be avoided. With some guidance from DMH, Len laid out the body lines of what was to become the most classic of the company's products. An innovation for us was the all-metal body. The body frame was made from steel tubing and sheet metal instead of ash which had been used on the previous models. Abbey Panels of Coventry built the aluminium skinned bodies at a price of £150 each.

The car's roadholding and handling were very good by the standards of the day. The maximum speed was less than either the Saloon or the Roadster models, 100 mph being just obtainable under favourable conditions. However, its handling was much more forgiving and it did not break away at the rear as readily as the Saloon.

We built a total of 100 Silverstone production cars, in two batches of 50– the D type and the E type. For the E type DMH thought up an original hood fixing, to replace the nailbreaking 'lift the dot' fasteners. A bar was stitched into the flat edge of the hood, which fitted into a curved extension to the top of the windscreen frame. This was easier to fix and also much more weathertight. We later resuscitated this method and used it in a modified form on the later MkI Sprites. All the production Silverstones were equipped with Adamant steering gears, while the works competition cars had special Burman steering gears, resulting in less backlash and lower steering effort. Unfortunately, it was not possible to use the Burman box in production, as we would not afford the tooling costs.

The front suspension of the Healey, which contributed much to its good road-holding, was an expensive and not entirely reliable assembly. On the A type the suspension boxes used to distort, causing a loss of camber. The B type boxes were reinforced but it was always difficult to keep the camber within

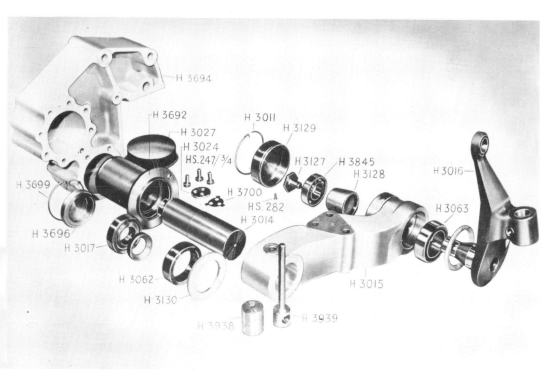

Front suspension parts for the Healey and Nash Healey. This must have been one of the most expensive front suspensions ever used on a production car.

design limits. For the C series Len Hodges worked a new box assembly. In place of the steel boxes, he arranged two heavy gauge steel plates with a large cast elektron spacer. The elektron castings were chemically treated to inhibit corrosion. The plates and bolts were zinc plated and assembled with a coating of Duralac. Very little corrosion problems were experienced with this design and the suspension settings were always well within design limits. Today, suspension incorporating ball and needle roller bearings using aluminium alloy arms and elektron spacers only appears on competition vehicles. This was a very costly assembly and today is a much admired feature on the Silverstone, where it is in plain view. We were still obsessed with the theory that wheels must rise and fall without camber change to avoid gyroscopic reaction and kick. Little did we realize that the very much cheaper Austin front suspension could be made to give better results.

One could sit in the Silverstone and see the front wheels and suspension working, which was intriguing until one came to a patch of road where a herd of cows had passed earlier. With the elbows-out driving position, one's right elbow would be liberally manured. A good old fashioned despatch rider's coat or driving coat was an essential part of the Silverstone owners's gear. In the days before restricted speed limits, I travelled long distances at night between Warwick and Cornwall at great speed and perfect safety. Because of the car's lighter weight the front suspension bearings lasted much longer than on the heavier four-seaters.

DMH and Ian Appleyard drove the prototype Silverstone, JAC 100, in the 1949 Alpine Rally, finishing second overall. In August of the same year three cars driven by Tony Rolt, Louis Chiron and Tommy Wisdom carried off the team prize in the production car race at Silverstone itself. Tony Rolt finished fourth behind two XK120 Jaguars and a Frazer-Nash. Many drivers served their racing apprenticeship on the Silverstone and a good proportion were also exported to the USA, where Briggs Cunningham, Phil Walters and Jim Rutherford had a number of successes racing them.

We made several attempts to increase the speed of the car, which with its 104 bhp Riley engine was barely capable of a top speed of 100 mph. We fitted one Silverstone with a Wade supercharger but limited development prevented it being a success. This car was exported to the USA and sold to a Mr Goodwin in Georgia. Briggs Cunningham's engineer, Bill Frick, had given a number of different cars an engine transplant, using the Kettering-designed Cadillac V8; the best known of these was the Fordillac, a Ford with a Cadillac engine. DMH obtained one of these new light Cadillac V8s and with advice from Bill Frick on what to use in the installation, we engineered its fitting into a Silverstone. Using a Ford gearbox and axle obtained from Soans of Leamington Spa, Roger Menadue, our experimental engineer, had the job done within a week. I tested the car around our Warwickshire test route and it was very promising. The silky smoothness of the V8 and its tremendous torque gave it a very high performance. One problem was transmitting the power to the road. I accepted an invitation from the Cornish Club to run it up Trengwainton, a hill climb on the Bolitho Estate near Penzance, at their Easter meeting. Of course on the appointed day the hill was reduced to a slippery slope not to the liking of the Cadillac Silverstone. Astley Cleeve with his Morris Special and someone with a 7 litre Hispano Suiza proved quicker.

We considered running the car in the Mille Miglia and Bassi, a very good Italian Mille Miglia specialist, came over and tried it out with me. He liked it but considered that the top speed was too slow to give it any chance of winning the race. The project was abandoned and the engine and chassis were sold to Portugal, the body being used for service purposes. Its demise was speeded up by the agreement to make the Nash Healey.

DMH had gone to America to try to obtain Cadillac engines from General Motors, travelling on Cunard's best ship, the *Queen Elizabeth*. On board he met George W. Mason, the President of Nash Motors, now the American Motors

The Cadillac-engined Silverstone at Trengwainton, Cornwall. The lights came out from under the bonnet to assist cooling.

A wet and slippery Trengwainton was not the best place to try the Cadillac-engined Silverstone.

Corporation. George Mason invited him to come to Kenosha and look at their products. The most powerful Nash engine at that time was the 3.8 litre Ambassador 6 cylinder, a straightforward unit of pre-war origin. As a result, Nash shipped over one engine, gearbox and rear axle for us to build into a car. Meade F. Moore, Vice President of engineering, handled the technical back-up from Kenosha. The original plan was for the units to be fitted into a Silverstone. Len Hodges, Barry Bilbie and I did all the design work and the car was assembled at the Cape. The Nash units resulted in a higher quality of ride and road holding than that given by the Riley units. The Silverstone now had more rear wheel travel, while damping was also improved due to the fitting of large diameter Girling rear dampers. We used Lockheed brakes—11 inch diameter by $1\frac{3}{4}$ inches wide for the front, and 10 inch diameter by $1\frac{3}{4}$ inches wide for the rear, together with Mintex M15 linings. These proved entirely satisfactory, no doubt because of the built-in air brake effect of the bodywork.

DMH and I decided to drive the car the 250 miles to Perranporth over the Easter holiday. However, despite cold and wet, it overheated and lost water within the first 50 miles. So we returned to the Cape and called out Roger Menadue. We decided that the cooling water was passing down one side of the radiator and Roger then added an extra inlet on the opposite side of the header tank. With two hoses from the top of the engine, the problem was cured. So we drove to Perranporth and back on the Easter Monday.

DMH and I took the car to Italy for the 1950 Mille Miglia Race. There, at the Sampietro Grand Hotel Tremezzo, I had the good fortune to meet my

Working on the prototype Nash Healey in the FIAT garage in Como, prior to the 1950 Mille Miglia race: Dunlop Mac, GCH, FIAT mechanic and Roger Menadue. The garage had an excellent machine shop and the usual competent Italian mechanics.

The prototype Nash Healey – a Silverstone with Nash units and faired-in wings – ready for our first attempt at Le Mans, 1950. The car finished in fourth position overall, driven by Tony Roth and Duncan Hamilton. Left to right: Percy Spooner (electrician), Jock Reid (experimental mechanic), 'Willie Migg', (mechanic).

wife Margot. The Italian petrol supplied for the race was of extremely good quality, having a far higher octane rating than the fuel we had used to test the car's performance back in England. In an effort to obtain more power we now decided to raise the compression ratio. So, with the aid of the Grand Hotel's chauffeur, Andrea Pini, I got the heavy cast iron cylinder head off and he drove us to the excellent FIAT Garage at Como where they had a very comprehensive machine shop. Margot speaks perfect Italian and was able to instruct the garage on the machining work we required.

Rebuilt, the engine was a little more responsive but the maximum speed increase was only just measurable. Harry Costley, Nash Motors' European representative, was travelling with us and it was thus important that we put up the best possible performance in order to retain his enthusiasm for the project. For the race, we were placed in the large sports car class and started very late among the big fast cars. The first portion of the race is on flat fast roads and whilst we could hold our own on the bends and hills, the Italian Ferraris and Maseratis left us on the straights in a most discouraging manner. In addition, using full throttle most of the time caused the water and oil temperatures to soar to alarming heights, although we did not use any water. Some 300 miles from the finish we were obviously not doing at all well and realized that some reason for our poor performance would need to be invented. We could not admit that the car was slow. In a deserted area we scraped the car along a wall. The first scrape was not enough but the second made a really convincing mess. As we rushed on to the finish we thought up a story, ending up with the tale that we had left the road and been fortunate enough to be rescued by a group of wandering monks who lifted the car back on to the road. Back at Calino after the race, our press friends questioned us about the incident somewhat sceptically. Basil Cardew, Courtenay Edwards and Tommy Wisdom knew DMH's capabilities as a driver and that it was most unlikely for him to have left the road. However, they kept the secret of the car's poor performance.

Our next competitive outing with the Silverstone was Le Mans. For this race, we decided to lose the air drag caused by the separate wings of the Silverstone and instead fair them into the body. Bill Buckingham did the metal work for us, and the maximum speed rose dramatically, to 124 mph. At Le Mans we were again accompanied by Harry Costley. Harry had a somewhat limited knowledge of racing and during the race was continually moaning about the fact that the car was not leading the field. On the Sunday morning he arrived at the pits and proceeded to groan away to Roger Menadue, saying that our performance simply was not good enough. Roger had suffered quietly, but this was too much for the hard working and patient man. He turned on Harry and exploded: 'You greedy bugger, how can you expect your old fashioned pushrod six to go quicker than all the hand-built twin cam racing engines?' I think that I was as surprised as Harry at this outburst, but Harry then saw the performance of the car in its true light and became more enthusiastic. In fact, Tony Rolt and Duncan Hamilton took the car to fourth place overall, winning the first Motor Trophy to be awarded by *Motor* magazine for the first British car.

With the improved speed of this body, the idea of a Silverstone powered by Nash units was dropped and Nash agreed to the development of a new car. Len Hodges designed a body and Gerry Coker blew up the $\frac{1}{4}$ scale drawing to full-size over a long weekend. This car became the Nash Healey, of which 250 were built at Warwick and a further 253 with bodies constructed by Pinin

Farina at Turin. The Silverstone was in essence a stop gap design, with a style of pre-war origin that was almost a classic when it was first introduced. Today, its unique form and small production have made it a much sought after model for restoration, despite the vast sums of money required to replace the bearings and shafts of its front suspension. The Silverstone did not contribute much profit to the company, but it helped its survival and, perhaps more importantly, helped to establish the Healey name in the USA.

When the time came to design the first of the Big Healeys, the Healey Hundred, the Donald Healey Motor Company was in good shape, due to the Nash Healey contract. All the profits we had made were then used to develop the new car. Our team at this time consisted of chassis designer Barry Bilbie, body designer Gerry Coker, works manager Harry Brandish, service manager Geoff Price, experimental engineer Roger Menadue assisted by Jim Cashmore, Bill Hewitt and Theo Goerres, toolroom experts Doug Pitkin and Bill Jarvis, workshop foreman Reg Muir, and trimmer Horace Fisher. Theo, a U-boat man and ex prisoner of war, later set up his own specialist machine shop. Purchasing was under the control of Bob Boardman, while Fred Draper ran the stores. I was in charge of engineering and design, while my brother Brian

John Fitch and Ray Wilday on the starting ramp for the 1953 Mille Miglia. The bodywork was cut away in an attempt to keep the drum brakes cool. The rear axle gears wore out after 200 miles.

MR. DONALD HEALEY, chairman, Donald Healey Motor Co., Ltd.... designer of Austin-Healey automobiles... Man of Distinction

Latest "M.O.D." is dean of international sports-car designers

If you haven't already guessed, the car is the record-breaking Austin-Healey "100". The man is Donald Healey, famed the world over for his ability to combine sports-car roadability and performance with arm-chair comfort and economy. The drink is Lord Calvert, which has an international reputation of its own. If you haven't yet tasted Lord Calvert, you've been missing a most pleasurable drink. One, in fact, that has made many people say: "It's true! You can't buy a better whiskey than Lord Calvert."

LORD CALVERT...FOR MEN OF DISTINCTION

The Austin PR organization arranged this advert with Lord Calvert. It caused some pretty acrid correspondence, the strongest being from our non-drinking relatives.

Where Austin Healey started: Earls Court International Motor Show, 1952. Len Lord of Austin and DMH look pleased with the deal they made.

or Bic joined us to sell the Austin Healeys to a great number of US servicemen. A great proportion of our skilled workforce had learnt their trade in Coventry, one of the great centres of the motor industry, while many had also been at Triumph before the war.

One always imagines that small is beautiful and that everything runs smoothly in a small company. This was not always the case, and there was a fair amount of bickering and backbiting. By the time the Austin Healey was in full production, there was time for people to squabble. Partly to make sure that we were more than fully occupied, but mainly because he was always impatient to start something new, DMH now started thinking about getting a new project underway.

A New Breed
of Car

The Sprite was first conceived in the winter of 1956, the result of a meeting between DMH and Leonard Lord. We always maintained a close relationship with BMC at various levels and DMH attended fairly frequent policy meetings. During a discussion on the sports car market, both men agreed that sports cars were becoming expensive, and that the market was contracting as the price went up. In his blunt, down to earth manner, Len Lord then commented that what we needed was a small, low cost sports car to fill the gap left by the disappearance of the Austin Seven Nippy and Ulster models of prewar fame. What he would really like to see, he said, was a bug. It is impossible to tell whether he was simply thinking aloud, or deliberately giving DMH a broad hint of what we should do, but this conversation certainly set DMH thinking as he drove back from Longbridge.

When he arrived back at Warwick, DMH called me in and told me the gist of his discussion, then proceeding to outline his own ideas about a small, low priced sports car. What we did not then know was that Austin had already drawn up a car to this sort of specification–the 7 hp two-seat Sports Tourer, designed in 1953. This car was neither very sporting nor much of a tourer. It had a tubular frame chassis, expensive in mass production, with no doors and a number of costly features. Although it in no way fitted the bill, we were to hear continuing rumours about it as the Sprite developed. In fact, I did not see a drawing of its general arrangement until spring 1978, when Peter Cahill kindly lent me a copy.

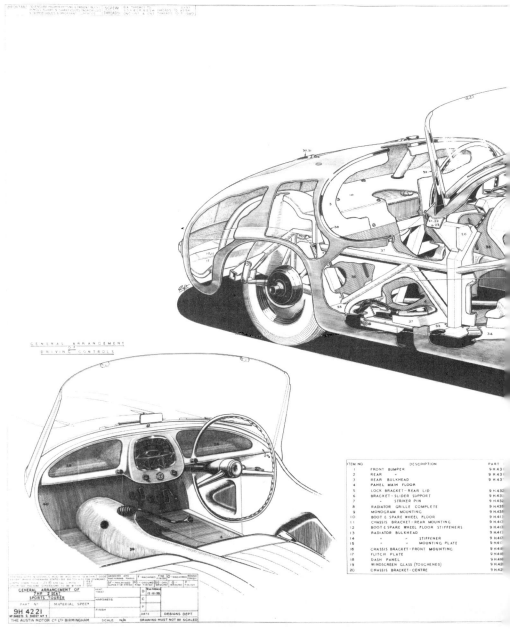

1953: Austin's proposal for a 7 hp 2-seater sports tourer. You could not get in or out with the hood up!

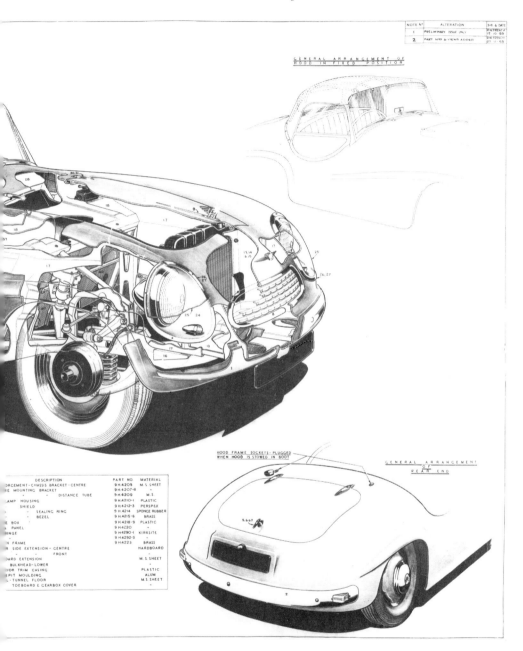

After my discussion with DMH, I was left with a lot of sketches and the OK to design and produce two prototypes. One idea was to make a car with a nearly identical front and rear end. Although this is possible, the end result is never pleasing and we did not pursue it. My first move was to ring Geoff Cooper at Austin and let him know what we needed. He had been appointed by Austin's chief engineer, Johnny Rix, in 1952 to liaise with us on all matters. He was to carry out this function with complete efficiency throughout an association lasting eighteen years. He always warned me not to take two bites at the cherry, and to order more rather than less of what we might need.

Three days later Geoff turned up with a car full of drawings, specifications and data, which we carried into my office. This was located on one side of the workshop, with only a coal burning stove providing a somewhat erratic heating system. Geoff also brought his list of individual component weights, a most useful document. He told me that the project had been cleared by his boss and that I was to let him know when we needed the bits.

I next told Barry Bilbie, our chassis designer, and Gerry Coker, our body designer, what we were going to do, at the same time emphasizing the need for the utmost security. I had decided that we should use the A35's front suspension, and engine and the basic case and track of its rear axle, with a 4.22 to 1 ratio. I had rejected the mechanically operated rear brakes of the A35, however, as these were not completely trouble-free and the installation would have presented some ground clearance problems. Instead, I decided to go for all hydraulic brakes. Lockheed calculated the brake performance and recommended suitable cylinder sizes, while the combined clutch and brake master cylinder came from another MG model. It was quite remarkable what performance was obtained with these small and light 7 inch diameter brakes.

We soon had a basic chassis layout which was to develop into the long running Sprite/Midget platform. When this was presentable we range Jess Bromley of John Thompson Motor Pressings who made most of our chassis frames, including those for the Austin Healey. He came over and discussed the design with us. Thompsons were interested in making the frames and agreed to deliver two within six weeks, for a nominal charge of £50 each. Barry and Wally Neale produced the necessary drawings very quickly, which were sent down to Thompsons in batches. In all there were some fifty-five separate parts in the under-structure though only very simple tooling was required.

At the same time, Gerry Coker was developing the body-lines to meet DMH's approval. From a quarter scale drawing he produced one to full scale on a 20 by 6 foot piece of paper pinned up on a hastily constructed wall board. From this full size layout Mr Sprang of Birmingham produced the wooden buck for the panel makers to produce the panels. The making of the prototype bodies was entrusted to Panel Craft, another Birmingham firm. Birmingham, England's second city, and its surroundings has always had a vast number of skilled engineering companies staffed by some of the hardest working and most skilled men in Europe.

Before long we were assembling the Austin units into the first frame, which was to be built up as a running chassis. One snag was the steering layout. We attempted to use the A35 steering gear but it quickly became obvious that little of the Austin stuff would suit. This meant that we would have been back with the old problem of six ball joints, an idler and steering box all adding up to indirect and vague steering. Instead, we took the Morris Minor rack and pinion and laid this in position. It was soon apparent that this set up would be superior, probably at not much extra cost. Once we had determined the correct position and checked that the steering geometry was good through the various wheel movements, we had to get some special steering arms made up. Jack Merralls, our Warwick blacksmith, made us a pair in EN16 steel which were then heat treated by the local gasworks. These were filed to the finished shape, drilled and fitted. Roger Menadue built up a twin carburettor installation, using the manifold off an MG model which he cut and welded to fit, while Jimmy Vincent of SU provided a pair of suitable needles and adjusted the carburettors. In a very short time we had the running chassis ready for testing. DMH and I drove it over our favourite short test routes through Barford to Wellesbourne and back, and found that it handled very well.

The first body was delivered by Panel Craft and fitted to the second frame. Lucas men Stan Glover and Jack Meddings came over to deal with the electrical side, giving us the simplest and cheapest electrical set up, including the direct acting pull starter solenoid. This pretty basic but effective electrical system was to give the Sprite the utmost reliability.

Sports car drivers like to have good instrumentation so that they can get the best out of the engine without abusing it. One of the most useful instruments is a tachometer or rev counter, but with the oil pump being positioned on the back of the camshaft it was difficult to find somewhere from which one could be driven. Our friends at Lucas and Smith finally solved this problem by providing a dynamo with a drive at the rear and an appropriate gearbox to give the instrument its correct drive ratio. This set-up provided a very effective indication of engine speed and also showed up a slack dynamo belt by giving a very low reading. Some trouble was later experienced in service when these little gearboxes seized up. This was quickly traced to ham-handed mechanics over-tightening the nut that held the box on with a large pipe grip.

One of the features of the first prototype were its pop-up headlamps. The car was very low and the headlamps had to meet a British regulation of 26 inches between the lamp centre and the ground. This ruled out any possibility of fitting the lamps conventionally in the wings. The two lamps were fixed onto hinges joined by a tube and activated mechanically so that they would swing up and forward to their operating position. When not in use, the lamps lay

The first Sprite prototype, Q1, with the bonnet off. The radiator and separate header tank were revised for production and the chrome plated pillars for the windscreen were replaced with painted ones. These changes showed a cost saving.

back flush with the bonnet. Unfortunately, in conjunction with the one-piece bonnet hinged at the back, this mechanism proved too complex and expensive, and was installed only on the first prototype.

The rear suspension consisted of two quarter elliptic leaf springs and two Armstrong dampers with long arms forming the upper torque reaction members. The aim was positive axle location with low unsprung weight. Everything was kept as simple as possible. The seat frames came from the Austin Healey 100, with greatly cheapened trim, while the external door hinges were very similar to those used on the 100 boot or trunk. All the locks and hinges were provided by Wilmot Breeden. The first prototype was finished in Dockers Carmine, a cellulose paint with a good red colour.

Known affectionately as the 'Tiddler', the car had not yet been given a name – merely the type number Q, this being the next letter in the chassis book. The first prototype was thus Q1. We always considered the name to be important and DMH spent some time thinking up various alternatives before he finally decided on 'Sprite'. All model names are registered with the Society of Motor Manufacturers and Traders and 'Sprite' was originally owned by Riley. It was just one of a great selection they had thought up, such as Imp, MPH, Gamecock, Alpine, and so on. Riley had used the name on one of their excellent sports cars before relinquishing it to Daimler, who were thinking of

Q1, showing the pop-up headlights, hand-made radiator grille with Austin Healey badge and the Sprite name on the bonnet. For production, we revamped the lamps, badges and hinges, saving costs and improving appearance.

using it on one of theirs. DMH made a few discreet enquiries at Daimler and was told that an approach from Austin would almost certainly be received favourably.

DMH and I did most of the initial development work on the prototype on the main roads of England. We had a number of favourite test places and hills. The straight level road near Coventry known as the Blue Boar Straight was used by most local manufacturers and in fact Rootes, now Chrysler UK, had surveyed it and painted quarter-mile markings on convenient trees. Here it was possible to obtain reliable quarter-mile standing start acceleration figures against the stopwatch. Another straight we used was the Bicester-Oxford road where tests for maximum speed could be conducted safely. Standing start tests for clutch suitability were carried out on the steep Edge Hill in Warwickshire. A popular test hill was Bwlch-y-Groes, in Merionethshire, which was long with very little traffic. Other pieces of road were selected because their surface formation provided a quick means of testing steering and the effects on handling.

I did a few runs with Harry Ladd, Armstrong Patent's resident damper engineer at Longbridge, to determine some damper settings. These were provisional of necessity, as the final setting would have to take into account the ultimate weight of the production cars.

Passing Geoff Price, I leave the Cape Works in the first prototype Sprite for a test run. Note the exterior door hinges.

Warwickshire County Council had an unfortunate habit of resurfacing any rough road section where damper assessment was carried out. This type of road work was later switched to the Motor Industry's Test Ground at Lindley, near Coventry, the imposition of a general speed limit on roads and improvements to the test facilities combining to make this a more satisfactory venue.

When we were developing the prototype, Peter Collins paid us a visit and DMH asked him if he would like to try it out. Peter was then one of the four outstanding drivers in Europe, the others being Moss, Fangio and Mike Hawthorn. I got in the passenger seat and Peter raced off into the country-side, going through the bends at speeds far greater than I used. After a bit I asked where we were going. He replied, 'I want to call on a girl I know in a village near by.' 'Do you mean so and so?' I asked. When he replied in the affirmative I told him that she had just married one of our salesmen, so the route was changed. Peter was very enthusiastic over the handling of the car and could hardly believe that it was based on the A35 units. For a Ferrari works driver, as he then was, he had surprisingly few criticisms of its concept and execution.

DMH finally pronounced himself satisfied with the prototype and rang up George Harriman at Longbridge, telling him that he had something to show him. Leonard Lord was now gradually handing over control of BMC to George, who had been made managing director and deputy chairman of the group earlier in 1956. He had had a long and successful career with the British motor industry, joining Morris Motors in 1923 and moving to Austin in 1940, becoming production manager in 1944. He was a very successful production man and a great deal of BMC's capabilities in this sphere could be attributed directly to him. He finally became both chairman and managing director in 1961.

George told DMH to bring the car over on 31st January 1957 and to put it in the garage under the Kremlin—this being the nickname of the head office block at Longbridge. DMH and I duly drove over on the day, cleaned off the mud and showed him the car. After a thorough inspection, he was obviously impressed and said that he would like Sir Leonard Lord to see it on his return on 20th February. Whilst Harriman was by now effectively running BMC, Len Lord still liked to be consulted. He, too, approved the car and it was decided then and there that Austin should make it under the type number AN5. DMH and Harriman agreed on conditions for its manufacture, while I drew up a provisional parts schedule and produced an estimate of costs. My figures came out to within £2 of those produced by Austin and, with the planned selling price of £450, promised an excellent profit per unit.

We now had to do a certain amount of redesigning and then provide Austin with the working drawings. We were in difficulties over the body engineering, as Gerry Coker was going to the USA, leaving us without a body engineer. DMH suggested that Les Ireland, who had worked with him at Triumph before the war, would be the ideal man for the job, and he joined us on 1st April.

Originally, it was planned that the new car should be built on the Austin A35 line at Longbridge. However, on this line the engine and axle units were offered up from underneath the body: to have this method on the Sprite would have entailed altering the front engine bay and chassis members, resulting in a wider car. Various schemes were prepared but after discussions with Austin it was agreed that to change the design to suit the available Austin facilities was not the correct procedure and that the original layout was more satisfactory.

It was decided that production of the chassis frame should remain with John Thompson Motor Pressings and that the Pressed Steel Company should tool up to produce the body at Swindon. Fortunately, they had a gap in their tooling programme and were able to slot the simple design into it with very little delay. Pressed Steel were and still are one of the best building companies in Europe, supplying Rolls-Royce and Jaguar among many others. They later joined with BMC and Jaguar to form British Motor Holdings.

The assembly of the new car was finally assigned to Abingdon, as it was decided that Austin would be fully committed with the revolutionary Mini design of Alec Issigonis, which was to replace the A35. Production of its transverse engine and the gearbox assembly would also keep Austin's engine men busy, and so the Sprite engine became the responsibility of Morris Motors' engine department at Courthouse Green, Coventry. Development thus fell into the capable hands of our old friend Eddie Maher and his team.

Once these decisions had been made, the busy Austin planners quickly laid down the production procedure. The chassis frames would travel from John Thompson's at Wolverhampton to Swindon, where Pressed Steel would press and assemble the bodies to them. The complete structures would then be painted at Morris Motors' paint shop at Cowley: their paint process was pretty well the best in Europe and complaints about the paintwork on Sprites were to be very very few. Indeed, the number of Sprites still in their original paint after twenty years of service is striking proof of this. From Cowley, the bodies would be sent to the MG factory at Abingdon, where they would be fitted with the engines, built by Morris Motors at Coventry.

With its single down-draught Zenith carburettor, the standard 'A' series A35 engine gave 34 bhp at 4750 rpm. We needed over 40 bhp. We filled Eddie Maher in on the background and he began work. While it is relatively easy to tune one engine to give a specified horsepower, it is much more difficult to obtain the same power from an engine produced in quantity. Eddie also had to subject the engine to a series of endurance tests, to ensure that it would have a satisfactory life span. Although the A35 was an excellent unit, the extra output and the hard treatment it would receive at the hands of sporting drivers called for some improvements. High quality bearings and an uprated clutch were thus fitted for the Sprite. After Eddie's initial development work, the 'A' series engine as used in the Sprite gave 42.5 bhp at 5000 rpm, with a torque of 52 lb/ft at 3300 rpm on a compression ratio of 8.3 to 1. With a bore and stroke of 63×76 mm, its capacity was 948 cc.

Test bed work on the power unit was followed by road development and proving. However good the work on the test bed, it is always necessary to make adjustments to carburettor settings to suit the installed conditions. Peter Knight and his team at SU Carburettors, another BMC company, were involved in determining these road settings, while the engine's cold starting was checked in the cold room at Lucas.

Meanwhile, our old friend Syd Enever now had another of our designs to look after at Abingdon. Though MG would naturally have preferred to have a car of their own design, Syd spared no effort in making the Sprite a success. In fact, MG had been considering a number of ways of producing a new, low-cost sports car of their own. One such idea was to revamp the MGA with A35 units, but the additional weight would have given this a considerably inferior performance to that achieved by the Sprite, and at much higher cost.

Les Ireland updated Gerry Coker's full size drawing, substituting internal hinges for the external ones, with a saving in cost. The complicated headlamp

The power unit of the Sprite, as shown in the press kit prepared for the announcement of the car.

mechanism was now scrapped in favour of a less costly system that was to give the car its bug-eye or frog-eye look. The body was widened slightly and built-in cowls were added to the bonnet, into which were fitted the same Lucas head lamps. More changes were made in consultation with the Austin body engineers. They felt that some of the body panels were unduly heavy and substituted thinner gauge sills and inner wings at the rear, more in line with those used on the A35.

The second prototype, Q2, was now completed, incorporating these modifications and thus adhering more closely than Q1 to the production design. This car was tested continuously and used to try out various improvements, such as a new radiator and heating system. This was kept simple, the ducting forming part of the chassis. Tom Haig, MG's test driver, put in an incredible mileage in a very short time. Part of the test work was an endurance run on the pavé track at the Motor Industry Research Association's testing ground at Lindley, not far from Coventry. Constant running over the pavé for up to 1000 miles provides

From the press kit: the rear suspension of the Sprite, showing the cantilever quarter-elliptic spring, torque arm and shock-absorber. We used the same Clayton Wright rubber mounting for the exhaust system as that fitted on the 100.

a measure of the structural strength of the body and suspension components. Any body that stands up to this sort of treatment is pretty certain to be satisfactory for use in all road conditions. Conversely, failure does not necessarily mean that a structure is unsound: a number of European cars with excellent reputations start breaking up after a very few miles on the pavé.

The preproduction Sprites showed a weakness around the rear suspension attachment and in the rear wheel arch area. The outer sills were coming off the tools in a slack or flabby condition and the amount of loose metal in the panel aggravated the distortion. The sills, rear wing panels and rear wheel arches were accordingly upgraded from a thickness of 0.036 inches to 0.048 inches, and the sill tools were adjusted to produce taut panels. With some additional gussets, we were now back to the specification used on the Q1 prototype! Cars built up with bodies incorporating these modifications were retested by Austin. They survived over 1000 miles of the pavé track and also showed a 30 per cent improvement in torsional and beam strength.

We also redesigned the rear suspension, incorporating separate upper torque reaction arms and lever arm dampers. The torque arms were simple pressings, fitted with Metalistic rubber bushes. These were one of the best types available, made by part of the Dunlop organization.

One might think that these development troubles were excessive, but this was not the case. A clear test run would simply have meant that either the tests devised were not sufficiently severe, or that the vehicle was grossly overstrong and heavy. However much development goes into a new model, some problems are almost bound to crop up, and not only at the start of production. Even Ford, the most efficient motor company in Europe, have their problems, while aeroplanes, with four engines and the most comprehensive servicing routine, are by no means infallible.

Austin had stipulated a very tight schedule in which to get the car into production. Again, one might say that it was too tight, although I think that if more time had been allowed the pace would have slackened and there would have been little improvements made. The original target date for the press release was 5th April 1958, but as this would have clashed with the announcement of a new Ford model it was put back to a free day—20th May. Cars

A Sprite chassis as prepared for exhibition purposes by MG.

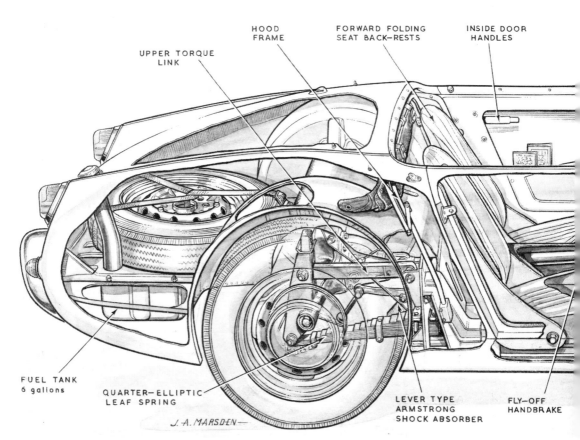

HOOD
FRAME

FORWARD FOLDING
SEAT BACK–RESTS

INSIDE DOOR
HANDLES

UPPER TORQUE
LINK

FUEL TANK
6 gallons

QUARTER–ELLIPTIC
LEAF SPRING

J. A. MARSDEN—

LEVER TYPE
ARMSTRONG
SHOCK ABSORBER

FLY–OFF
HANDBRAKE

The original Sprite—another splendid cutaway drawing published by Autocar.

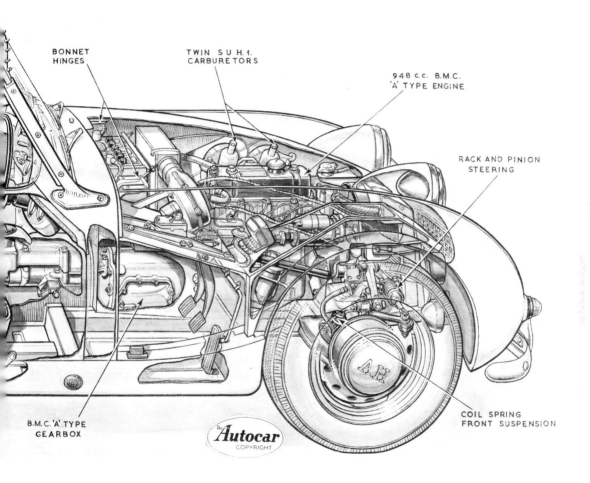

BONNET
HINGES

TWIN S U H.1.
CARBURETORS

948 c.c. B.M.C.
'A' TYPE ENGINE

RACK AND PINION
STEERING

B.M.C.'A' TYPE
GEARBOX

COIL SPRING
FRONT SUSPENSION

The first catalogue announcing the Sprite.

were coming off the MG production line at Abingdon in March, the first chassis number being 501. The target selling price was raised by £5 to £455, plus an iniquitous £224 purchase tax on all cars sold in the UK.

Despite the vast number of people who had looked at the new model and offered numerous criticisms, suggestions and comments, we still forgot to provide an ashtray – though not many owners complained!

Frog-eye:
an Instant Success

DMH naturally wanted to have the press test the Sprite under conditions that would really show up its virtues. One advantage of the date fixed for the announcement–20th May 1958–was that it coincided with the Monaco Grand Prix. This meant that a large number of motoring correspondents for the national press would be gathered together in Monte Carlo, with easy access to roads which were ideal for demonstrating the Sprite's excellent handling–and under Mediterranean sunshing to boot.

MG undertook to deliver a supply of the cars to Monte Carlo, while Jim Bramley–BMC's sales director, Reg Bishop, Sam Haynes and John Bowman organized and prepared the necessary press material. DMH also arranged for our own yellow Sprite, YAC 740, equipped with a slightly tuned engine, to be taken over, as he and Tommy Wisdom intended to try it out around the old Mille Miglia race course in Italy. This was the first time such a big gathering had been arranged to test one of our products and I was asked to come along in case any technical points were raised, about which my knowledge would prove useful.

A lot of the press, the Austin men and myself gathered at Heathrow Airport for a flight to Nice on one of British European Airways' excellent Vickers Viscounts. On the flight we were each provided with a well produced folder of press information, including some excellent photographs taken by BMC's photographic department under Ron Beach. Thus, by the time we reached our destination, the press men had a pretty good idea of what to expect and

Reg Bishop, in charge of publicity at Austin, with Tommy Wisdom and DMH, all looking pleased with the way the press preview was going in 1958.

were eager to get to work. A short bus ride took us to the hotel at Monte Carlo where a line of gleaming Sprites took everyone's eye. The press men paired themselves off and set off for a hard day's driving around the roads rising above Monte Carlo. The day was warm and sunny and meticulous planning ensured a thoroughly enjoyable outing for all concerned. Only one of the cars misbehaved, when a throttle cable came adrift. All the time and expense that had been put into the operation was more than vindicated when the press reports came out, for there was nothing that fell much short of a rave notice.

Tommy Wisdom in *Sporting Life* called the Sprite 'the first ever people's sports car', going on to comment that 'the feature that will amaze and delight all who drive this model is the leech like road-holding. I have never driven a safer faster car.' In the *Daily Herald* he called it 'the spring-heeled Sprite'.

In the *Daily Telegraph*, W. A. McKenzie wrote: 'my conviction is that the makers who have laid down complete tooling for large scale production will find ready buyers for every model they can turn out.'

The *Manchester Guardian* contributed the only real criticism, considering the Sprite's headlamps to be its only fault: 'They appear to have been added as an after thought and they sit rather uncomfortably on the bonnet.'

In the *Daily Mirror* Pat Mennem announced that 'a new nippy little sports car—the sort that big manufacturers have not marketed since before the war—makes its appearance today.'

Laurie Cade in the *Star* reported that 'suspension is excellent, road holding surprisingly good, the engine is flexible and the brakes are powerful. Indeed it is just the job for those who have not been able to afford this type of car.'

Jack Hay devoted half a page to the Sprite in the *Birmingham Post*: 'Without doubt, this car is a winner. There is a considerable demand in Britain for this type of vehicle—a small car that is safe and lively.'

Daily Mail motoring correspondent Courtenay Edwards described how the Sprite caused a sensation wherever he took it. 'The Sprite is one of the prettiest

The press men pair off for their test drives in the new Sprites at Monte Carlo in May 1958.

May you meet many smiling faces in 1959

This was drawn by Brockbank, the celebrated motoring cartoonist, and was used for DMH's 1958 Christmas card. When the Sprite was first introduced, an American journalist referred to it as 'The car with the smiling face'.

and perkiest little two-seater touring cars that has ever come out of a British factory. It is the sort of car many thousands of motorists have been waiting for. It will – mark my words – start a new motoring vogue in Britain.' His newspaper subsequently ran a contest, offering six Sprites as prizes.

Pipe-smoking Alan Brinton of the *News Chronicle* called it 'an exciting new little sports car' and generously forebore to include his caustic remarks, made in Monte Carlo, about the lack of an ashtray. How we missed this important item I cannot think!

Basil Cardew, doyen of motoring journalists, noted five outstanding points in the *Daily Express*:

'1. Roadholding better than any car I have tested.
 2. A top speed in the 80s – remarkable for so small a car.
 3. A petrol thirst that ranged from 35 to 50 miles to the gallon according to the speed.
 4. Get there quick acceleration.
 5. Roominess of the two bucket seats.'

In conclusion, he wrote, 'I believe that this cheap but most efficient sports car, the Sprite, will prove to be a big seller—here and abroad.'

The Times gave a large piece to the car: 'The Sprite is so well balanced and has such high geared, positive, and light steering that it is an unusually pleasant and safe car to drive in these extreme conditions of successive hairpin bends. On ascents the engine seemed to revel in hard work and high revolutions in third and second gears, while going down hill the brakes were sound and fully in keeping with the character of the car.'

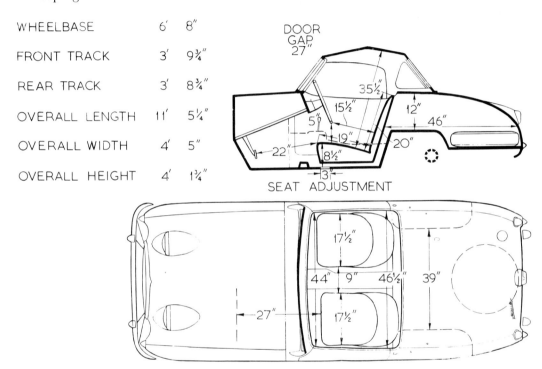

WHEELBASE	6'	8"
FRONT TRACK	3'	9¾"
REAR TRACK	3'	8¾"
OVERALL LENGTH	11'	5¼"
OVERALL WIDTH	4'	5"
OVERALL HEIGHT	4'	1¾"

The interior dimensions of the MkI Sprite. For a small sports car, it had a large luggage boot.

Gordon Wilkins in the *Observer* commented that 'unlike most British cars it oversteers, but the tendency for the tail to drift outwards is easily checked by the quick steering, which needs only two and a half turns from lock to lock and is unusually reluctant to spin the inside wheel on sharp corners.

'In the rain the weather protection is very effective and at Monte Carlo we were amused to find that the tail holds more luggage than an Italian convertible costing ten times the price.'

PBL 75–probably the most photographed Sprite of all. It was sometimes left-hand drive.

'At £455 it will consolidate Britain's position as the world's supplier of sports cars at reasonable prices which no other country has yet been able to challenge.'

Ian Nickols in the *Sunday Times* found the Sprite enchanting. 'I drove it several hundred miles, not because I had to, but because I wanted to. Even more surprisingly, my wife wanted to come with me.'

The *Glasgow Herald* hailed it as 'a significant new British car', while the *Buxton Advertiser* considered it 'worthy of praise'. In the *Western Mail*, Harry Drake dubbed it 'a Sprite with an elfin look – and a bite'.

Two full road test reports were issued, one by *Motor* (number 15/58), the other by *The Autocar* (number 1688). In both cases, the car used was PBL 75, which must be one of the most photographed cars of all times. *Motor* headed their report 'Motoring that is fun at very modest cost', and commented that 'were it possible to define quantitatively a pleasure-to-price ratio for cars, the new Austin Healey Sprite would undoubtedly register an amazingly high figure for this virtue.'

In all, we filled over 80 pages of our cuttings book with press announcements on the Sprite. It is sad that many of the newspapers and periodicals from which these came no longer exist.

It is impossible to quantify the effect of publicity upon sales, but with the Sprite the response from the press was immediately followed through in the salesrooms. The public's reaction to the car was overwhelming and sales were buoyant from the start. With the introduction of the Sprite, numerous enthusiasts were at last able to afford a true sports car. We had always thought of it as a car for the young, but in fact many elderly people also went out and bought one, to recapture the joys of the motoring days of their youth. Sammy Davis, one of the greatest drivers and Le Mans winners of the 1930s, bought one of these early models and thought highly of it.

By 1959 Sprites were arriving in the USA in sizeable numbers and BMC decided that some additional publicity, geared to this most important market, would be advantageous. This took the somewhat unlikely form of a record breaking expedition to the Bonneville Salt Flats in Utah. By 1959 record breaking was really played out—the public had already seen a series of attempts, going back to the 1953 Austin Healey runs—but BMC nevertheless decided to set up a new expedition for September, primarily to put a very special MG record breaker through its paces. This had been designed at Abingdon by Syd Enever to attack international class records for short distances up to 10 miles, at speeds of over 250 mph. Unlike all BMC's previous record breakers this car was not based on a production chassis and consequently its shape was dictated only by the need to produce very low air resistance. With the engine set

Sprites on the Austin Healey stand at the 1959 Motor Show.

Tommy Wisdom in the MG-built Sprite record breaker EX219, talking to Alec Hounslow of MG's development department. Alec spent most of his working life at MG, building prototypes and specials.

in the middle, driving a de Dion type axle with a track of only $38\frac{1}{4}$ inches, the car was a mere 38 inches high. The driver sat well forward with his feet some 20 inches in front of the front axle.

An outing to Bonneville is a costly operation and it was decided that to take another car along for an additional series of records would not have much effect on the total outlay. Syd Enever therefore designed another record breaker based on an MGA chassis frame and fitted with a blown 950 cc Sprite engine. This car was very similar to the famous MG record breakers used earlier by Goldie Gardner. 189 inches long, 41 inches high and $63\frac{1}{2}$ inches wide, the car was quite a bit longer than a Sprite, though of course its air drag was very low. With a full fuel tank and a driver on board it scaled 2114 lb against the 1901 lb of the MG car. The engine was blown by a Shorrock supercharger, a creation of the brothers Noel and Chris Shorrock, an eccentric vane type often used for record breaking.

BMC's publicity handout prior to the attempts stated that: 'The record attempt is essentially an endurance test of the Austin Healey Sprite, BMC 950 cc 4 cylinder "A" series engine. The engine and gearbox are in most respects

The cockpit of MG's Sprite record breaker, EX219, showing the nice clear instruments provided by Smiths.

quite standard, such as cylinder block, head, crankshaft and all other details. The few special parts, such as pistons, valves, valve springs and clutch, are the same as can be obtained through BMC Service Ltd for competition tuning of the standard "Sprite". To obtain the additional power required for these high speeds an ordinary "Shorrock" low pressure, belt driven, supercharger kit is fitted. This gives a manifold pressure of 6 to 7 lb per square inch and the engine will produce 78 bhp at 5500 rpm or 86 bhp at 6000.

'For the 12 hour record we shall be using approximately 70 bhp at 5400 rpm for 135 mph, using a 2.88 to 1 rear axle ratio.

'So that we may also attempt a short distance sprint record at maximum speed, a spare engine is available, with a slightly higher compression ratio (otherwise it is identical to the 12 hour engine) developing 98 bhp at 6500 rpm, with which it is hoped we shall attain 145/150 mph.'

It is now history that the MG, EX 181, took International Class F records with its 1500 cc engine, and with its 1506 cc engine took International Class E records from 1 kilometre to 10 miles distance. The drivers were Britain's Stirling Moss and America's Phil Hill. EX 219, the so-called Sprite, was driven by our old friends Tommy Wisdom, Ed Leavens and Gus Ehrman. Ed, a

Canadian, and Gus, an American, both worked hard selling our cars in North America. The three drivers broke many International Class G records, from 50 kilometres at 145.56 mph to 2000 kilometres at 138.86 mph, and so the Austin Healey marque was credited with another batch of records to add to those held by the 4 and 6 cylinder cars. Naturally, Dunlop provided the special tyres and Castrol the lubricating oil.

All BMC's publicity for this event, and indeed the very reasons why it was staged in the first place, assumed a somewhat naive public. This assumption was false, for in fact sports car owners are among the best informed members of the motoring public. The car bore little resemblance to a Sprite and the sports car buying public were not very interested in it. Its effects on the sales of production Sprites was thus pretty well negligible.

The original Frog-eye model continued in production for three years with

Wood rim steering wheels were an option available from Warwick. We later became aware of the dangers of wood splinters in an accident and used Paddy Hopkirk's excellent leather-covered wheels.

little more than detail improvements. Optional equipment was made available both from our organization at Warwick and from BMC. This included Shorrock supercharging kits, similar to that used at Bonneville, large numbers of roll bar kits, which we had designed for the car in the prototype stages, and some rather noisy exhaust systems. MG designed a hard top for the car which was built by Jensen as a solid fibreglass moulding with a toughened rear window. Although expensive, this was of extremely high quality and was often used on competition cars. Towards the end of the period of Frog-eye production we also supplied wire wheel kits and disc brake conversion kits. Tuning equipment was available from a variety of independent tuners who had previously produced the power for the A35 saloons. Unfortunately, a number of so-called tuners did nothing but extract money from those owners who were unfortunate enough to use their services. To some people, a snorty exhaust note and a rough engine seems to indicate performance.

By early 1961 sales for the car had started to decline. Although this was probably due to general market conditions, BMC decided that a face-lift was now necessary. In America, the rule of annual model changes was well estab-

The Healey disc brake and wire wheel conversion kit for the Sprite. The master cylinder and hose assemblies are not shown. Wire wheels later became a production option.

lished, the theory being that it was desirable to introduce some visible difference to persuade people to change their cars. The distinctive Frog-eye lamp
treatment had been a constant source of criticism, as had the one-piece lift-up
bonnet. Today, of course, it is these same features which give the original
Sprite the status of a collector's item.

In all some 49,500 Frog-eye Sprites were built, including a number assembled overseas from 'completely knocked down' kits supplied by BMC.
In spring 1961, when the original model was due to run out and the new model
about to appear, Austin's sales organization decided on a campaign to sell the
now obsolescent Frog-eye. National Sprite Week, as it was called, was the first
time any major sales campaign had been mounted for the Sprite. Within days
all the dealers were out of stock and clamouring for more. Even today one
cannot be sure whether the MkII Sprite, and the subsequent marques, were
strictly necessary. I certainly could go no further than to say that it was to be
a mixed blessing.

Dual Development of Sprites and Midgets

The decision to produce a new model of the Sprite was the signal for another concentrated spate of development work, both at Warwick and at Abingdon. After a series of meetings with Austin, we were given some loose guidelines for producing a new front end. Back at the Cape factory, DMH, Les Ireland and I started preparing a scheme. This Les drew up to full size and it was then mocked up in modelling clay for DMH's comments. After Ted Eves had taken some photographs for the record, we moved on to producing the steel panels. One of our primary considerations was to ensure that the minimum of alterations would be necessary to the rest of the body.

We had been told not to talk to MG about what we were doing, but part way through Syd Enever rang me and told me that he had something to show me. I arranged to meet him at Morris's body branch at Coventry, where we had a somewhat guarded conversation about what was going on. It transpired that Syd was producing a new back end with Eric Carter at Coventry. He felt that we ought to get together, as he was worried that his design might not have agreed with our own. Since Syd had been officially informed of our own development work, I was more than happy to reveal to him all that we were fabricating! As a result, we were able to produce a much more uniform design than would have been possible if both sides had continued to work in complete isolation.

The next move was for all the drawings to be sent to Pressed Steel at Swindon for the wooden tooling models to be made. This was the first time the new front

The prototype MkII Sprite, still retaining the MkI tail, with an air scoop offered up for viewing by DMH. Photographed at the Cape by Edward Eves.

and rear ends went together. There was some dispute over the front wing crown line. Blending this into the unchanged scuttle panel presented quite a problem, but after a couple of visits to Swindon this was eventually resolved to everyone's satisfaction. From then, on, Syd bore the brunt of the work needed to get the car into production. The extent of the alterations to both front and rear ends was such that tooling costs for the new model exceeded the total costs of the original car.

The main changes to the front of the car were to the bonnet, which was now separate, to the front wings, on which the head lamps were positioned conventionally, and to the radiator grille. The rear deck behind the seats was also cut away, to form additional luggage space. We had already made this modification to a number of Frog-eyes, at DMH's instigation. The MG-designed tail included a separate lockable boot and more substantial bumpers. Although many people did not agree with the change in appearance, the new model did possess certain practical advantages. The bonnet was much easier to lift, being

Tommy Wisdom zooms uphill in the 1959 Targa Florio. With co-driver Bernard Cahier in the MkI Sprite 7080 AC, he finished a creditable seventeenth overall in this classic event. Expert photographer and journalist Edward Eves has captured the atmosphere of Sicily in this photograph.

Gerry Coker drew up this styling scheme for an A30-engined sports car in 1952. When we came to design the Sprite four years later, we considered that this type of car would be too expensive.

We kept trying to make the Sprite look more sporting. An egg box grille, simple bumpers and separate side and indicator lamps were one idea produced by our stylist, Doug Thorpe.

Mk II Sprite prototype, showing the MG-designed rear end. The line of marks down the side of the car is where the trim strips were fitted when the same car was photographed as the new Midget.

lighter, and the locking luggage boot and additional space behind the seats did make the car appeal to a wider market.

The chassis and running gear were identical to those of the Frog-eye, but the 948 cc 'A' series engine had now been improved. The crankshaft was strengthened, and a new camshaft was fitted, with a longer exhaust opening period and increased valve lift. The larger $1\frac{1}{4}$ inch HS2 SU carburettors were fitted, and the cylinder head was improved with larger inlet valves and double valve springs. The compression ratio was raised from 8.3 to 1 to 9 to 1. These modifications increased the power output to 49.8 bhp at 5500 rpm, while the stronger crankshaft made the engine run much more smoothly.

While the MkII Sprite was being tooled at Swindon, George Harriman – the king of badge engineering – decided that there was a good reason to make an MG version of the car. Although BMC had a high degree of integration in the manufacturing field, Morris and Austin retained their separate marketing

Badge engineering. BMC used the MG name on a version of the Issigonis designed 1100 and made a determined effort to sell the MG 1100 in the USA, but America was not then ready for small front-wheel-drive sedans. Note the use of the Healey plate on the Austin Healey 3000.

and dealer networks. The Morris organization was very strong on the sporting car side, with its MG and Riley marques. Many of these dealers and distributors had been selling MGs since the marque first began and were much more interested in sports cars than their Austin counterparts. They had always envied the Austin dealers when they had the Sprite, and were delighted at the prospect of a new, low cost sports car. In George Harriman's opinion, although an MG model might initially depress demand for the Sprite, there would be a significant increase in total sales, with two different marques being sold through two separate franchise networks.

It was agreed that the MG Midget should be introduced at the same time as the MkII Sprite, in May 1961. The Midget was to retail at a slightly higher price and its radiator grille was accordingly graced with vertical slats, a traditional hallmark of the more expensive car. Apart from the badge, the only other difference between the two models were some stainless steel trim strips, which were fitted to the bonnet and sides of the Midget as an identification mark.

The performance of the two cars was identical, with a top speed of 86 mph –

BMC's press release for the USA. The body strips on the MG tended to cause rust to develop. This unnecessary feature of badge engineering is no longer used on today's Midget.

BMC's press release for the UK. Comparison of the two press releases reveals the external differences between the Midget and the MkII Sprite.

FUN FUN NEW
NEW
NEW FUN FUN
FUN
SPRITE
FUN FUN FUN

BMC has the inside track on outdoor fun! Loads of fun, lots of fight, might and muscle ...that's the Sprite! Odes to sports cars are rare. Rare too, is a car like the Sprite. It's the lowest priced <u>true</u> sports car in America; it's a race-bred Sebring champ; it's a frisky, audacious little rascal that roars like a lion and pivots like a cat! It's a <u>pleasure</u> car to drive; in teeming traffic or down a shady lane. And it's made by BMC ...builders of the sleek MG, and the sizzling Austin Healey. Test drive the fun-tastic Sprite at your nearby BMC dealer's today.

Represented in the United States by

HAMBRO AUTOMOTIVE CORPORATION, LTD.
27 W. 57TH ST., NEW YORK 19, N.Y.

From Safety Fast, *August 1961. BMC's advertising of the Sprite was up to their usual high standard, emphasizing the fun side of the car.*

SHE
CATCHES THE EYE
FROM THE WORD "GO"!

THE NEW ⬛MG⬛ MIDGET

THE CAR THAT *Starts ahead*

The great M.G. Midget is back again! In top form, the modern version of a classic—and with magnificent lines! Here's a thrill — a *safe*, delightful thrill. For what is safer in motoring than high performance through the gears, wonderful braking power and the great M.G. assets of firm road holding and stable cornering? They're all here! The new Midget quite literally *has* got *EVERYTHING*.

SPORTING TRADITION

B. M. C. RESOURCES

ABINGDON CRAFTSMANSHIP

Safety fast!

**WITH A SPORTING APPEAL
FROM A SPORTING ANCESTRY**

M.G. MIDGET Price £472, Plus £197.15.10. P.T.
P.T. figure is subject to a 10% surcharge

*12 Months' Warranty and backed by B.M.C. Service—
the most comprehensive in Europe*

THE M.G. CAR COMPANY LIMITED, SALES DIVISION, COWLEY, OXFORD
London Showrooms: Stratton House, 80 Piccadilly, London, W.I.   *Overseas Business:* Nuffield Exports Limited, Cowley, Oxford and 41 Piccadilly, London, W.I

From Safety Fast, September 1961. BMC carried out separate sales and advertising campaigns for the Sprite and the Midget.

BMC's production hardtop for the MkII Sprite and Midget followed MGB lines.

3 mph faster than the Frog-eye. The 0 to 60 mph acceleration time was advanced 3 seconds, to 30.6 seconds. Before too many owners start gunning for me, I should add that these small engines showed some variation in power output. Performance normally improved after 5000 miles had been covered, particularly after the back axle had been worn in. When new, the back axles consumed some power and ran very hot.

Two further models were introduced under the BMC banner at the same time as the MkII Sprite and Midget–the MkII MGA 1600 with the 1622 cc engine, and the MkII Austin Healey 3000 with three SU carburettors. (Production of both the Healey models was initially in left-hand-drive form for export, as stocks of the Frog-eye and the MkI 3000 had been allowed to run out, in anticipation of the changeovers.) To introduce four new sports cars simultaneously was quite some achievement. The basic UK retail prices of the cars were: Sprite–£505; Midget–£515; MGA–£663; and 3000–£824.

Twelve months after the introduction of the Midget and the MkII Sprite, BMC uprated the 'A' series engine. The bore and stroke were now increased to 64.85 mm and 83.72 mm respectively, giving a capacity of 1098 cc. These early 1098 cc engines were not very popular: the crankshafts were relatively weak and spindly, and the engine felt rough at speed. Whilst still bearing the designation MkII, Sprite chassis numbers were allotted a new prefix, AN7.

At the same time, Lockheed disc brakes were introduced, on the front wheels. At Warwick, we had been using disc brakes for a long time, fitting first Dunlop and then Girling experimental disc brakes to the Austin Healey special test cars in 1953, and pioneering the use of disc brakes on the production 100 S cars. Towards the end of the period of Frog-eye production, we had started to supply Girling disc brake conversion kits, again for the front wheels only, as an optional extra. Girling had been granted a licence by Dunlop, the

A Warwick-produced hardtop on the MkII, designed by Les Ireland. It was lighter than the BMC type and gave improved visibility. Quite large numbers were produced.

inventors of the disc brake system, and had subsequently developed a production version which was copied in many countries. These were extremely good brakes and we would have liked to use them on all the production Sprites and Midgets. Unfortunately, this would have conflicted with BMC's model policy, which specified Lockheed as the suppliers for all 'A' series units (i.e. cars of 948–1098 cc capacity) and Girling for the 'B' series (cars of 1500–1622 cc). Thus we had to use Lockheed units.

The design of the Sprite's front suspension and steering meant that it was impossible to fit a large diameter disc without modifying the shock absorber and steering arms. Using a small diameter disc presented us with another problem, for with no servo we were forced to use high friction brake pads. Over the years, the brake lining manufacturers, and our old friends Mintex in particular, have made great strides in reducing pad wear, increasing friction coefficients, improving stability with temperature variation and increasing fade resistance. At that time, however, brake pads with high friction co-efficients did not wear well and would not stand high temperatures. The early days of disc brake development were exciting, for this new device was so far ahead of the existing drum system. Due mainly to the conscientious efforts of our experimental staff under Roger Menadue, and brake men like Ken Light and Tony Cross of Girling, I experienced only one case of brake failure during this development work – and that was caused by a design fault, which was quickly rectified.

Numerous tests were carried out both at Warwick and at Abingdon before a satisfactory set-up was devised for the Spridget. Although the pad problem was not entirely eradicated, the Lockheed system, with its very small diameter discs, coped very well with normal sports car motoring when fitted to the production cars. It only revealed its shortcomings when used on the very much faster racing cars.

The MkII Sprite/MkI Midget remained in production until March 1964, when they were replaced by the MkIII Sprite/MkII Midget (the Midget was always one mark number behind, as it was introduced with the MkII Sprite). The new models were powered by an improved version of the long stroke 1098 cc engine. The main bearings were increased from $1\frac{3}{4}$ inches to 2 inches, and the increased strength of the crankshaft made this a much happier unit than its predecessor, and also more amenable to tuning. The cylinder head was also improved, with better porting and larger inlet valves.

During the intervening three years, since the introduction of the MkII/MkI Spridget, we had concentrated our development resources upon improving the car's ride comfort, and the weather protection afforded by the hood assembly. These were the two features of the car which were most frequently criticized, and as a result of this work the new models incorporated important modifications in both areas.

Although the original Sprite design, with its quarter elliptic cantilever rear springs and torque arms, was eminently suited to the original concept of a very basic sports car, it did not provide a degree of ride comfort compatible with the more sophisticated vehicle the Spridget had since become. This deficiency, due mainly to the lack of rear wheel movement, was exacerbated by the higher weight of the MkII series, which tended to make any shortcomings in the car's handling show up more prominently. We had always suffered from lack of wheel movement with the cars we designed. In the planning stages, we would try to ensure ample bump and rebound movement, but body and development work usually resulted in this being decreased. Despite our spring makers' confident assertions that their springs would not settle, being made of the finest material and within their specified stress limits, some settling in invariably occurred.

In searching for ways to increase rear wheel movement and thus improve the ride, both MG and ourselves came to the conclusion that the quarter elliptic springs would have to be replaced by the more conventional half elliptic type. This would entail deleting the torque arms, which in turn meant that the springs would subsequently be responsible for absorbing all the torque reaction.

The M.G. Car Co. Ltd. Sales Division, Oxford
Overseas Business: Nuffield Exports Ltd.,
Cowley, Oxford & Piccadilly, W.1

12 Months' Warranty and
backed by B.M.C. Service—the
most comprehensive in Europe.

J2 Midget! What memories it conjures up! Based on the magic Midget, holder of every International Class H Record in its day and many others besides. Such was the ancestor of your present Midget. M.G. enthusiasts build them now, as they did then, to match your enthusiasm. The Mk II Sports Convertible has fully wind-up windows and adjustable quarter lights, lockable doors with exterior handles, curved windscreen, new suspension, increased power, new de luxe cockpit, plus the vast resources of B.M.C.

30 years on

Safety Fast **MG MIDGET** Mk. II Sports Convertible £515 plus £107.17.1 PT.

From Safety Fast, April 1964. BMC realized the value of the MG name and used the association of MG and the earlier Midgets in their companies – even to the extent of using the MGI plate on the car.

Mill Street, Warwick, used as the background for a MkIII Sprite publicity photograph.

For this reason, some people considered this development to be a step back-
wards, despite its other advantages.

The body construction of the Sprite made fitting the new springs a simple
matter. We fabricated front and rear mounting points and soon had a car
ready for testing. The new system worked well. Ride was improved, and the
removal of the torque arms, which had fed axle and road noise into the rear
cross member of the understructure, reduced the noise level in the car. As an
added bonus, MG were able to put the system into production at no extra
cost, as the springs were cheaper to produce.

Meanwhile, we were working on a scheme to provide the car with wind-up
windows and a hood attached to the body. With official backing from BMC, we
modified another MkII Sprite, under the code number SM4. We received a
tremendous amount of technical support from Wilmot Breeden—suppliers of
most of the window gear and locks used on British cars, and from Weathershields—one of Britain's best hood makers. Hood specialists are a dying breed,
but we were fortunate in that Les Ireland, our body engineer, was one of the

74

best around. A true master of this art, Les had been responsible for the excellent top used on the pre-war Triumph Dolomite Roadster among many others.

Les first drew up the frame mechanism full size and then constructed the linkage in thick card, with nuts and bolts for the pivots, to test the folding action. He then produced a metal frame and fitted it to the car. Slight adjustments were necessary to make sure that it went up and down easily, and that it locked together when erected, to form a rigid base. The hood covering was then fitted and the whole assembly was subjected to static test, followed by a road test of the car. Further modifications were necessary to ensure that the hood did not billow out, flap or rattle on the hood sticks and that it retained its fit around the side windows, excluding wind and rain.

This project resulted in a hood that was easily erected, provided excellent weather protection, and folded away below the body–but it was complicated, and the cramped space in the door would have posed problems in production. However, the exercise did prove that wind-up windows and a convertible hood were possible on a very small car like the Sprite. It also revealed that glass

MG improved and updated the dash panel and instrument layout for the MkIII Sprite. The next change of the panel was a backward move to meet US safety legislation.

wind-up windows with no draught vents were no more costly than aluminium framed sliding side-windows.

Once we had proved the feasibility of these improvements, Syd Enever undertook a production design at Abingdon, resulting in the MkIII/MkII Spridget with its convertible hood, roll-up side windows with no draught vents, and an improved windscreen. The tooling changes were not extensive, and the whole assembly was of a standard otherwise only available on very expensive luxury cars. The interior of the new models was also made more civilized than that of their predecessors. The instrument panel was improved with a speedometer and electronic rev counter positioned on either side of the steering column, angled inwards to improve visibility. A useful parcel shelf was fitted on the passenger's side, to make up for the loss of the door pockets which had had to be sacrificed to make room for the winding mechanism of the windows.

The importance we attached to the hood assembly can in part be attributed

SPRITE MK IV

Retained in two places on the windscreen head-rail, it is but a simple operation to unfasten the quick-release catches, whereupon the durable, vinyl-coated fabric hood can be folded down in a matter of seconds. When stowed, the hood is neatly enclosed in the tailored cover supplied as standard with every Sprite.

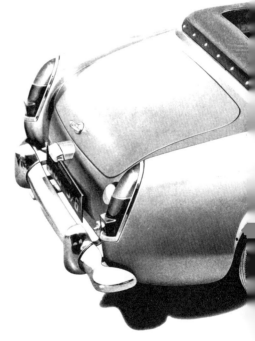

From the catalogue for the MkIV Sprite, extolling the virtues of its new hood assembly.

to a remark once made by American sports car buff, Tom McCahill. He referred to our Nash Healey hood as being made by a sleazy umbrella maker with the DTs. The memory of this certainly goaded us into trying harder, and we were to spend some time in the years between the MkIII and MkIV in perfecting the Sprite's convertible top or hood. The final assembly, as fitted to the MkIV Sprite/MkIII Midget, has always been considered one of the best ever produced for a small sports car. In fact, very few sports cars of any size ever provided the same degree of weather protection. The Italians were always thought to lead the field in the production of convertible tops, but even they were never able to equal the low cost unit of the Spridget.

The MkIV Sprite/MkIII Midget were the last of the range with which we were to be closely associated. Introduced in 1966, these models were powered by the 1275 cc 'A' series engine with Borg and Beck diaphragm spring clutch and Austin gearbox. With some twenty odd years of development and racing behind it, this unit represented the zenith of the production engine development

for the series. With a cylinder bore of 70.61 mm and a stroke of 81.28 mm, it was identical in size to the Mini Cooper S engine, but its power output was deliberately restricted to enable it to be manufactured from lower cost materials. The use of smaller valves and a lower compression ratio gave it a power output of 65 bhp at just under 6000 rpm. BMC claimed a top speed of 95 mph with a 0–60 mph acceleration time through the gears of 14 seconds, but it was a poor car that would not lap MIRA's banked test track at higher speeds after a little running in.

The 4.2 to 1 rear axle ratio was retained initially but was later replaced by the higher 3.9 to 1 ratio which improved fuel consumption and reduced engine noise at high cruising speeds. The crankshaft was also improved shortly after the new engine was introduced. Initially this was made in one of the normal BMC alloys but this showed signs of distress and was replaced by a nitride-hardened E40 steel. Though effective, nitriding proved too expensive a process and was finally rejected in favour of the similar but cheaper process of Tuft-riding. This resulted in a crankshaft of satisfactory strength, at an acceptable cost.

The price of the Sprite had risen slightly over the years, from £455 for the basic Frog-eye to £545 for the MkIV. The MkIII Midget was still £10 more expensive, at £555. Contemporary prices for other models in the BMC range were £642 for the Mini Cooper 1275S, £746 for the MGB Roadster, £865 for the MGB GT and £915 for the Austin Healey 3000. These were the basic retail prices, on top of which the Government imposed its purchase tax, which varied with the years. Available extras for the Spridgets included an anti-roll bar at £2, laminated windshield at £4, a tonneau cover at £6, wire wheels at £25, an oil cooler at £6.50 and a hard top at £50. The many improvements to the hood, resulting in the MkIV/MkIII version, led to a sharp decline in demand for hard tops.

During the summer of 1967, the sales department got in a tizzy over the Honda S800, a so-called sports car from Japan. Its outstanding feature was its 791 cc engine with a claimed output of 70 bhp at 7000 rpm, which could have posed a threat to the Spridget in world markets. We decided to put it to the test and borrowed two cars, one from Peter Wilks of Rover, and another from Lucas. The engine was very lively and if one was brave enough the car seemed to be very slightly faster than the MkIV/MkIII Spridget, though its roadholding and handling were diabolical. Of course, with its small capacity high revving engine, one needed to make full use of the gearbox. Its top gear acceleration figures were very poor in comparison to the Spridget's and it exhibited a frightening degree of bump steer that could catch out the unwary or a driver of limited experience. In fact, one of the English companies testing the car fitted a large notice warning drivers not to exceed 50 mph. However, it was possible that the Japanese might learn something about steering and

MIGHTY SPRITE

Mightier than the big boys.
Two class firsts and a second
at Sebring, outlasting many
of the 3 and 4 litre heavies.
Only British finisher at
Le Mans with all those
great big specials dropping

*The successful 1967
Austin Healey Sprite prototype*

like flies around it. That's some motor car. Come and see
what is developed from successes like these, at your Austin Dealer.

Austin Healey Sprite

1275 ccs of high performance for £671.12.4 including p.t. *(wire wheels optional)*
The British Motor Corporation Ltd., Longbridge, Birmingham.

From Safety Fast, *October 1967. BMC made good use of the Sprite's racing successes
to promote the car.*

handling, and should these defects be rectified it could pose a real threat.

It was agreed with Austin that we should borrow a production Midget and
carry out a series of tests, using the production engine, a Sprite engine tuned
to Cooper S specification, and another uprated engine prepared by Eddie
Maher which would have been less costly to produce and more economical
than the rather thirsty S unit. Rather than subject Peter Wilks's Honda to the
strain of taking a full set of production figures, we decided to use those published
by *Motor*. Both *Motor* and *Autocar* employ very competent road test staff and
use a standardized test procedure.

For some unknown reason, MG at first failed to send us the car, claiming
that all the tests had been completed. Austin were not satisfied, however, and
commanded MG to send it over immediately. We were fortunate that one of
the industry's best test drivers, John Harris, was not then gainfully employed

and we were able to obtain his services. He took the car over to the Motor Industry's Test Ground at Lindley near Coventry, where he spent a couple of days producing the figures. Mike Guest was responsible for carrying out the lightning changes of engine between the tests. The results make interesting reading, and are reproduced in the appendices, page 220.

The road holding and handling of the Spridget were always of the highest order and the tests proved that its performance would be superior to the Honda's were it fitted with the uprated engine. However, then the Honda threat disappeared–maybe a member of Japan's fifth column told them that we were more than ready for them! In a way, this was disappointing, because it meant that there was now no need to introduce the very potent unit developed by Morris Engines. I believe that in fact MG were none too keen on increasing the Spridget's performance, as it would then have got too close to that of the MGB.

Whilst we had effectively dealt with the Japanese threat, certain individuals within our own group now threw a spanner in the works. Some genius in America decided that in order to make the cars distinctive for the new model year, all external brightwork should be finished in dull black. Just how he managed to get this idiotic modification through, I will never know: it may have been simply because the USA was the most important market, and suggestions emanating from the States were always given great attention. The process used was a new German one, whereby an epoxy powder was baked onto the metal, resulting in a hard coating with very little brightness. The general effect was funereal and sales declined alarmingly as there were few undertakers wanting to buy Sprites or Midgets for their business. The later Spridgets were never beautiful, relying on attractive trim to add some character. DMH and the Austin sales people soon had the original brightwork restored, and sales picked up at once. This epoxy process was last used to finish the Jensen Healey bumpers, which were not exactly renowned for style or non-corrosive properties.

In 1968 the result of a lot of skirmishing behind the scenes was announced with the merger of Leyland and BMH to form the British Leyland Motor Corporation. In the short term, this had little effect on the production of Sprites and Midgets. Our consulting agreement with BMH still had some time to run and we continued to co-operate on the development of both production and competition cars.

After the merger, the Triumph men tended to look upon their Austin counterparts with a certain amount of scorn, acting the part of rather bumptious experts. This was illustrated graphically at one meeting, when we were discussing the old problem of gearbox noise. When we first designed the Sprite chassis structure, we made the tunnel and gearbox cover a close fit around the 'A' series box, positioning the top hat cross member to take the rear mounting. This was excellent for production and enabled the seats to be nicely positioned,

1968 Sprite with the dull black screen, grille and lower panel. This American-inspired treatment was not to our liking and was dropped very quickly. (Austin Morris)

but it did have a couple of flaws. It made it impossible to fit an overdrive unit, and it also magnified any gearbox noise. Although rarely objectionably noisy, Spridget gearboxes could never be described as quiet. This was a service problem and we all tried hard to reduce the noise without spending much money. At the meeting, the Triumph expert proclaimed that one could not make quiet gearboxes with aluminium casings, and that the problem would disappear if we switched to cast iron. 'Laughing Jackass', as he was known, certainly made a lot of noise. Needless to say, some cast iron casings were made up and the gearboxes built and tested, without the slightest improvement. The inability to fit an overdrive like the GKN Laycock unit in the Spridget was regrettable. This unit makes long journeys far more enjoyable, reducing engine fussiness and improving fuel consumption. Although we did fit an overdrive for competition use, the necessary modifications to the chassis structure meant that it could never become a production option. This feature must have gained Triumph a lot of sales at our expense.

In 1969 our long association with BMC came to an end and the following year British Leyland gave us notice that they were ending production of the Sprite. While we had earned consultants' fees on all the Sprites and Midgets produced at Abingdon up to that date, the terms of our contract did not cover any subsequent production of the Midget. It is easy to have hindsight and say that we should have drawn up a water-tight contract covering such a development, but sadly this was not the case. We thus played no further part in the development of the MG Midgets that followed.

Twenty years after the introduction of the Sprite, the Midget is still leading its field. It has grown heavier over the years, but this has been more than compensated for by the increase in engine size. With a capacity of 1493 cc

1975 Midget with its energy-absorbing bumper. (Austin Morris)

and a bore and stroke of 73.7×87.4 mm, the four cylinder engine of today's Midget propels the car at speeds comfortably in excess of 100 mph, with 65 bhp. It remains economical with over 30 miles to the gallon. Even today, the Midget retains the basic sill pressing of the original Sprite, with the curved top line at the front designed to suit the lift-up bonnet. Wall to wall carpeting and excellent seats now complement the Sprite hood. I drove one recently, with the happy owner sitting alongside to curb my exuberance. It was still a Sprite, with that direct responsive steering and safe handling, and I immediately felt at home in it. The impact absorbing bumpers do not improve its looks, but their mass does do something for the ride quality.

In 1978 the Midget costs £2395, over four times what it cost ten years before. Such is the price of inflation, for it is still the world's lowest priced sports car, serving to introduce many new owners to the unique joys of sports car motoring and perhaps whet their appetites for a larger car. After they have moved up to an MGB they are stuck, unless they are fortunate enough to be able to buy and maintain a Porsche or a Ferrari.

All credit for keeping the price of the Sprites and Midgets down, so that for some twenty years now they have given the public the cheapest form of sports

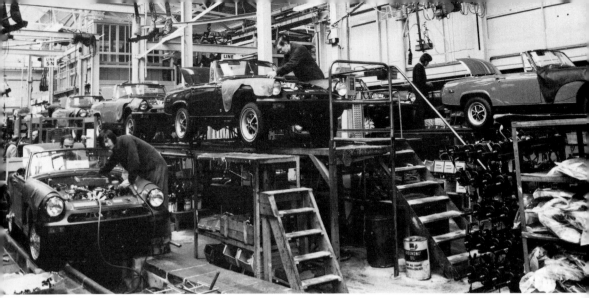

The latest MG Midgets on the production line.

car motoring, as conceived by DMH, must go to that great company MG at Abingdon (originally in Berkshire but now maddeningly in Oxfordshire!). Better to be small and shine than big and cast a shadow.

The Engines

The number of people who took to modifying the 'A' series engine at every stage of its development is pretty varied. Like all manufacturers, we were continually seeking more power and thus always on the look-out for any new system or technique which resulted in improved performance. Although some of these developments were dictated by the special needs of the racing cars, many others were subsequently incorporated in the production units and were thus of direct benefit to private owners. The man who probably made the greatest contribution to improving both the power and the strength of the 'A' series engine was Eddie Maher at Morris Engines. This was largely as a result of his work on the BMC Formula Junior engine, which continued until 1964 when the Cosworth-developed Ford engines ran away with the series.

The 948 cc unit fitted on the Frog-eyes and the early MkII/MkI Spridgets benefited from Eddie's work on the Formula Junior engine as used in John Cooper's car, with which Jackie Stewart did so well. This used the stronger crankshaft connecting rods and valve gear that were essential if the tuned unit was to stay together. The crankshaft was nitride hardened and manufactured from better alloy steel, and this found its way into most of our racing engines.

Harry Weslake, one of Britain's greatest independent tuning experts, was also involved with the 'A' series from the very start. He tuned one engine for us in July 1958, raising the compression ratio to 10.12 to 1, fitting two $1\frac{1}{2}$ inch H4SU carburettors and modifying the ports, to give 64.5 bhp at 6000 rpm. We fitted this to a Sprite and after our own tests submitted it to Austin. Gill

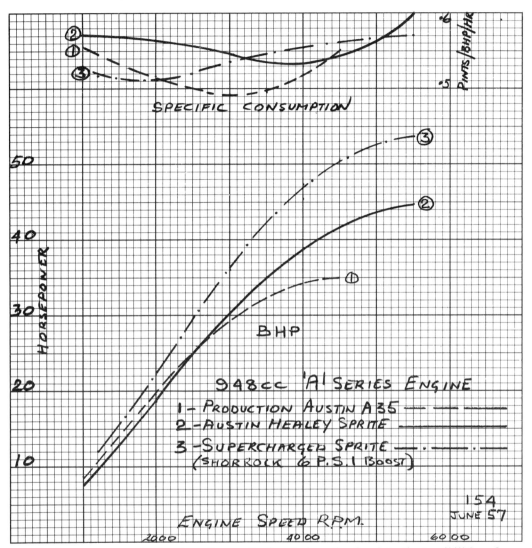

Performance curves produced as the result of early investigation into the possibilities of tuning the 'A' series engine for the Sprite. As the result of road tuning, the Sprite engine showed improved specific fuel consumption. Although almost a year away from production, we were already looking at ways of increasing the power output.

Jones and Harry Broom tested the car at the MIRA test ground, obtaining a lap speed of 98 mph and a 0–60 mph time of 15.4 seconds. What was really interesting, but not of great importance in the days of comparatively cheap petrol, were the steady speed consumption figures obtained from Harry's patented combustion chamber. In the table below, these are compared to Shell's figures as obtained from a production Sprite.

	Weslake engine	*Standard engine*
30 mph	72.4 mpg	57.2 mpg
50 mph	49.3 mpg	52.0 mpg
70 mph	38.8 mpg	42.9 mpg

A racing engine does not need to be thirsty and this type of consumption would go down well today. Harry Weslake was always very clever at making engines burn lean mixtures.

Harry came up with another suggestion for producing a special head, that would give us the power we required. He designed a single overhead camshaft unit that could be bolted to the standard block. Naturally the inlet and exhaust ports and combustion chambers were very special. However, just when the design was completed and pattern equipment about to be made, someone at Austin got to hear about it. Both we and Harry were politely told not to go ahead and that was the end of the matter. Just why this was done I never understood, but as both our companies were small, we could not afford to go too far out of line.

Tim Fry, then with Rootes, now called Chrysler UK, designed another interesting head with separate ports. This improved output with very little development but was never very reliable.

Outside Harry Weslake the most successful independent tuner was undoubtedly Daniel Richmond. He tuned a large number of A35 and Sprite engines, most of his checking being carried out on the road, against a stopwatch. He had the knack of producing more power without spoiling the tractability. Jim McManus, one of our London showroom managers, fitted one of his engines and exhaust systems to his own Sprite and I took a full set of figures on it. It proved particularly good in the 60 to 80 mph range but was somewhat erratic at low speed. Daniel worked closely with BMC on the 1275 cc Minis during the era when the Mini Cooper S really dominated the rally scene.

We spent some time experimenting with superchargers on the 948 cc unit, in conjunction with Chris and Noel Shorrock. We used a Shorrock supercharger on the so-called Sprite record car at Utah in 1959 and also supplied Shorrock kits for the Frog-eye Sprites. Supercharging engines was not a new concept, having been very popular on high performance cars in the thirties. One was always looking for some low cost option that could be bolted on to the engine with the minimum of skilled labour, to produce a greatly enhanced performance. When all went well, the Shorrock kit increased the Sprite's performance considerably, without too much detriment to fuel consumption, giving 57 bhp at 5700 rpm and 46 bhp at 4500 rpm. With a high degree of tuning, the installation could give up to 90 bhp for competition purposes, though this of course did use up a lot of fuel.

It was possible to increase the boost pressure up to a maximum of 6 lb per square inch, by changing the pulleys used with the belt drive from the crankshaft. Throttle response was good and the engine would pull strongly from low rpm right through the speed range.

There were a number of snags, however. Some of the production superchargers were not well made and badly balanced rotors gave rise to some nasty vibration. This caused frothing in the carburettors and wore out the needle valves, as well as being most unpleasant. Oil consumption was sometimes a problem. The oil supply to the supercharger was metered by a pin of different diameter to meet the requirements of individual units. The increased combustion pressure and temperature caused a small number of pistons to seize or pick up. We overcame this problem by fitting pistons with solid skirts, with greater clearance obtained by piston expert Cecil Winby from Brico in Coventry. We fitted these pistons to the supercharged demonstration car and once Chris Shorrock had adjusted the oil supply and carburettor we had a very reliable machine.

The formula applied to determine the class in which a supercharged car raced moved it up amongst much bigger machinery. Generally, the effect of supercharging is to make the car have the characteristics of a bigger engine. Mainly for this reason, we decided not to continue these experiments but to concentrate instead on normally aspirated engines.

The introduction of the MkII/MkI Spridget presented us with one new problem as far as racing was concerned. When Syd Enever and his men redesigned the rear end, they altered the rear wheel apertures to strengthen the body at this point. This change meant that one had to jack up the body and let the back axle drop in order to remove a rear wheel. It also made the fitting of oversize tyres difficult, often necessitating pushing out the wing and beating in the inner wheel arch. The Special Tuning Department naturally specified the use of Dunlop racing tyres for racing and we found that these could not be fitted safely without alterations to the bodywork. I wrote to Basil Wales, the head of Special Tuning, pointing this out, but was told that they were not able to test all the options they offered.

A further constraint on tyre size was to occur when the semi-elliptic rear springs were fitted on the MkIII/MkII Spridget. These springs were fitted with clips which were sometimes positioned where they could rub racing tyres on hard cornering. We used to specify clips of thin steel positioned where they could not gouge the tyres. The production clip with its rubber insulation was bulky and could reduce tyre clearance by $\frac{3}{8}$ inch. Removing the clips entirely would have been disastrous as the spring leaves would then have been free to shift about, and possibly cut into the tyre.

The 'A' series engine was increased from 948 cc to 1098 cc in 1962, twelve months after the introduction of the MkII/MkI Spridget. The weak crankshaft of these early 1098 cc units did not stand up to the rigours of competition. Quite a number of crankshafts broke under racing conditions and this made us decide not to use this unit in our own racing Sprites. Instead, running in the prototype classes, we were able to use a special short stroke 1098 cc unit developed by Eddie Maher and Derek Frost at Morris Engines. With a bore of 71.63 mm and a stroke of only 68.248 mm, these engines would run to high speeds with reliability, producing nearly 100 bhp. They were both strong and amenable to tuning, having been developed to counter the very successful Ford engines tuned by Cosworth, which were dominant in the Formula Junior. In addition to the short stroke 1098 we also raced a number of engines with a stroke of 76 mm.

In his attempts to get more power from the racing engines, Eddie Maher produced a variety of heads, including one very effective casting that had two separate exhaust ports for the two middle cylinders. We were able to fabricate exhaust manifolds with this feature, and as a result gained 3 bhp.

To have put the short stroke 1098 cc engines into production would have meant a considerable tooling investment. Instead, Morris Engines concentrated on developing the long stroke 1098 cc unit and an improved version, together with a stronger crankshaft, was introduced with the MkIII/MkII Spridget in 1964. For racing, the blocks were bored 1.5 mm, to bring the capacity up to 1143 cc, just inside the 1150 cc class limit. In this form it could be tuned to give close to 90 bhp and was quite successful. Dick Jacobs ran these units in the GT Midgets developed by Syd Enever at MG.

The stronger of the 1098 cc long stroke production engines could be tuned to give 96 bhp at 7000 rpm, though in this condition of tune it was really only suitable for short distance events. It took a lot of work to produce this power. The block had to be bored 1.5 mm oversize and recesses had to be cut to provide clearance for the exhaust valve heads. The valve seats had to be enlarged in diameter, the face had to have 1.5 mm machined off, the ports had to be ground out and the combustion chamber polished. Then one had to obtain an AEA648 camshaft, large inlet and exhaust valves, duplex chain and sprockets, bronze valve guides, special springs and collars and a Weber 45 DCOE carburettor with inlet manifold and the best exhaust system. The whole had to be assembled with great care. There is no cheap or easy way to obtain power.

Club member Gerry Watts, who worked for Magnesium Elektron, had some pistons produced in magnesium alloy for the 1098 cc 'A' series engine. These were considerably lighter than the conventional type, with no loss of strength, and enabled the engine to be run at much higher speeds. They were used suc-

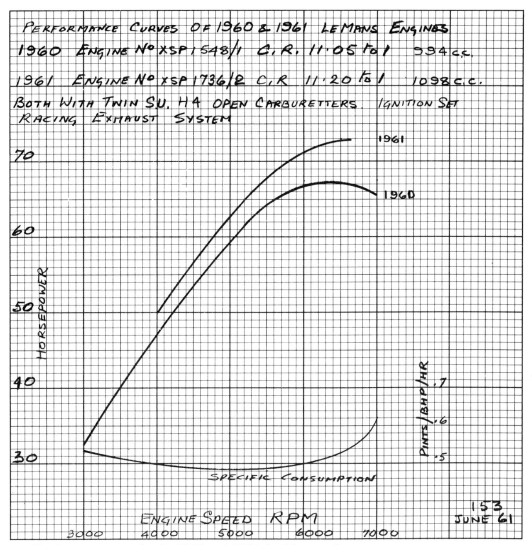

Performance curves for the 1960 and 1961 Le Mans engines.

cessfully in short distance events and showed great promise, apart from a tendency to develop cracks in the gudgeon pin area. Their development was abandoned just when they were starting to prove reasonably reliable. Sadly, Gerry Watts died in a motoring accident caused by a skidding lorry and trailer.

The 1098 cc engines were used in production for four years until October 1966, when the 1275 cc engine was introduced with the MkIV/MkIII Spridget.

For racing, we used a .5 mm oversize bore and pistons, giving a swept volume of 1293 cc–just nicely inside the 1300 cc class limit. Some of our failures with the early engines resulted in the stronger crankshafts being fitted to the production units.

Stretching the 'A' series engine from 803 cc through various stages to 1293 cc was not without a lot of problems. The larger engines tended to be rough and quite a lot of parts broke in racing. Most of the problems centred around the crankshaft. First we broke connecting rods, resulting in the introduction of much improved rods. Then we had troubles keeping the crankshaft in place. In addition, the production scroll type of oil retainer would leak considerable quantities of oil under racing conditions. This usually collected in the clutch housing and drained off at every pit stop. We tried all sorts of modifications to the scroll and drain pipe, but without success. Both types of problem were finally cured when we fitted a cast aluminium sump or oil pan, together with a special Angus oil seal at the rear of the crankshaft. The oil seal eliminated the oil leaks, while the extra rigidity obtained by bolting on a more substantial sump made the engine run more smoothly.

The rigidity of the assembly was further increased by fitting a five-speed gearbox, with its stronger connections. The basic design of the Spridget made it extremely difficult to fit an overdrive unit, and although we had fitted these on the competition cars in 1965, we had been forced to cut about the chassis structure in order to do so. In theory, even with 100 bhp engines the Spridget gearboxes were within acceptable stress limits, but in practice their life under racing conditions was short. To overcome this, it was decided at a meeting at Austin that we should use MGB gears in a new casing, and that Morris Engines should devise a five-speed box. This can be a satisfactory alternative to gearbox and overdrive, though most five-speed boxes have a rotten shift quality and often a difficult gate pattern.

Suitable casings that would fit the Sprite engine were designed, with the fifth gear outside the main housing. The shift pattern adopted had the normal one to four gear positions with fifth and reverse to their right. A positive lock operated by a plunger prevented accidental engagement of reverse. Eddie Maher sent us the first box so that we could let him know the exact spring settings, gear lever length and slope we wanted. I spent two days testing a variety of combinations until we got one that was perfect. The result was one of the most foolproof and easy to change five-speed boxes I have ever tested–and every box that Morris Engines produced afterwards was identical. In comparison the Getrag box used on the Jensen Healey was an abomination. More than usual attention was paid to the Sprite box as it was on the cards that we might have had it on production.

In competition, it is the very small increases in power that make all the difference to performance. One of the many ways to achieve such an increase

1293 cc Sprite racing engine, XSP2173-4, developed for Le Mans. Note the motor cycle clutch cable for the throttle, Weber carburettor, quick release cap on the oil tank at rear left and waterproof plug covers.

is to modify the exhaust system, and over the years we did quite a lot of development work in this field. The first competition exhaust system we built for the Sprite had two pipes from the outer pair and inner pair of cylinders carried right through to the rear of the car. It made a lot of noise and showed a small horsepower increase over the production cast iron manifold and system. The sales people loved these as they were sold in vast numbers as optional kits. Eddie Maher computed the critical lengths for the manifolds during his tests on various systems and sent us the figures and details. We found that the best system consisted of a manifold using $1\frac{1}{4}$ inch diameter tubing, the outer pipes being 10 inches long up to the point where they joined one another. At a point 23 inches beyond this, the pipe from the centre cylinders joined them in a Y piece, and from there back the tubing was of $1\frac{3}{8}$ inch diameter. This system gained 2 bhp at 4000 rpm over the two pipe system, rising to $4\frac{1}{2}$ bhp at 6000 rpm. We used this on all the works competition vehicles from 1961 onwards, to the annoyance of the sales and service departments who sold the lower power system in very large numbers. BMC's special tuning department subsequently put the improved system into production as an optional extra for all Spridget owners who wanted greater performance.

The later racing engines all had dry sump lubrication. A straight gear pump was fitted on the old petrol-pump boss and driven by a skew gear on the camshaft. This sucked oil and air out of the sump and through rubber oil pipes through a BMC oil cooler to the oil tank, located in the passenger foot well. We made these tanks in light alloy at Warwick, incorporating Wally Hassan's suggestions on how to separate the air out of the oil effectively. Inside the filler neck we had fitted prominent maximum and minimum oil level indicators. The cooled and de-aerated oil was fed to the normal pressure pump at the rear of the camshaft, which forced it through the filter to the bearings in the normal manner. The tank held a maximum of 2.9 gallons of oil.

This system held a pressure of 80 lb per square inch from 3000 to 7500 rpm. Pit stops were easy as on opening the cap one could see immediately whether oil was needed. One problem was that great care had to be exercised when starting the engine in cold conditions, as any excessive engine speed would cause a high oil pressure that blew out the filter sealing ring. Once the engine had been warmed up prior to a race, the pressure relief valve kept the pressure within safe limits.

Each year we claimed more power from the racing engines but the increases were never up to the claims. As the Sprite engines were built for long distance international races, they were not tuned to the same degree as the racing Mini Cooper S units, and on Morris Engines' advice we used a considerably lower maximum engine speed.

In 1968 we introduced Lucas petrol injection on our competition cars. Lucas made Roy Wood responsible for this development and he spent some time

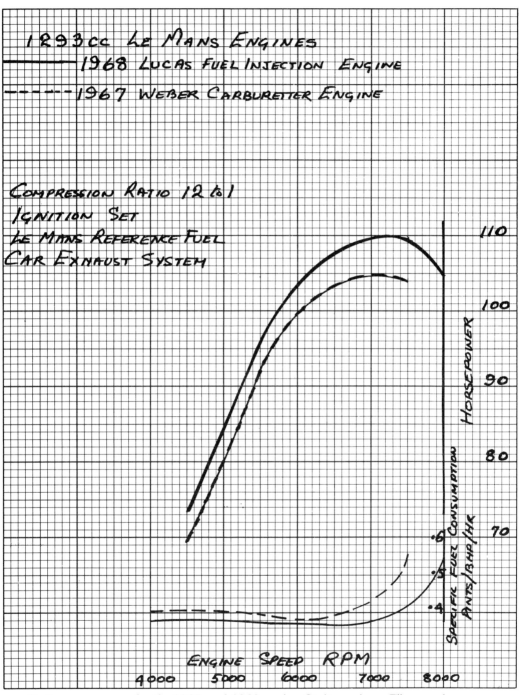

Performance curves for the 1967 and 1968 racing Sprite engines. These engines were built for long distance races. For sprint events, output could be raised by nearly 10 per cent.

The Lucas petrol-injected engine used in 1968 at the end of Sprite racing development. This was a wonderful system which we should have had years before.

with us, making sure that the installation was suitable. With the Weber carburettor, the engines gave around 105 bhp at 7000 rpm; with Lucas petrol injection this was increased to around 110 bhp at the same speed. We modified the tank to incorporate a catch tank from which the Lucas high pressure pump drew petrol, forcing it through a pressure regulating valve at 120 lb per square inch to the engine-driven metering pump. This metered the exact engine requirements to each of the four injectors at the correct time. The metering pump supplied fuel in response to throttle opening. The throttles were four SU butterflies in castings mounted on the inlet ports. A CAV fuel filter ensured that only clean fuel was delivered to the metering unit. The main supply pipes were Aeroquip high pressure petrol hoses and in addition there were spill return and excess pressure return pipes from the pressure valve. The system did not incorporate any form of cold starting enrichment, the normal procedure being to choke the intakes with a sheet of metal. This injection equipment on the Sprite engines worked faultlessly throughout some very long races.

As far as the Sprite was concerned, this 1968 series of engines represents the peak of development. If we had continued racing the power would have been increased to over 120 bhp.

Getting power is one matter, and making sure that the engine has a satisfactory life with that power is another. Much of the credit for the long life of today's engines must go to the suppliers of the pistons and bearings. The pistons used on the Spridgets were produced by members of the Associated Engineering Group, namely Brico and Hepworth and Grandage. We made great use of Brico's piston expert, Cecil Winby, to solve our problems. Our bearings came from both Vandervell, members of the GKN group, and Glacier. Vandervell were the originators of the thin wall steel backed bearing that replaced the old babbited white metal type and made it possible to achieve today's high outputs. They achieved world leadership in the bearings market as a result of their involvement in racing which continues to this day. Way back in the thirties, when DMH was in trouble with the bearings on the new straight eight Triumph Dolomite engine, he called on his friends at Vandervell. If you strip almost any British engine, you will find components supplied by GKN and Associated Engineering providing an unobtrusive service that outlives the foreign opposition. At one time, every mine had a Cornishman at the bottom of it. Today, most fine engines have Vandervell bearings at their heart.

After the Sprite was dropped from production, both the MG Midget and Spitfire continued to be exported to the USA. It would have been expensive and stupid to continue developing two very similar power units to meet the US emission legislation and so the 1493 cc Spitfire unit became common to both cars. With over 200 cc more capacity and four separate inlet ports, the Triumph unit in USA specification gives much better output than the 1275 cc 'A' series unit in equivalent tune. Its DIN ratings are 65 bhp at 5500 rpm in European form and 57 bhp at 5000 rpm in USA specification.

Everyone in the USA suffers from the effects of emission legislation, leading to heavier fuel consumption and loss of performance, but the Midget suffers less than most small cars. If it was not for emission controls people would now be driving more exciting cars with Lucas petrol injection.

Progress is a mixture of snakes and ladders. In 1959 the production cars had 43 bhp and the racing cars 57 bhp. In 1968 the racing cars had 110 bhp and today the production car for the USA has only 57 bhp. From Johnny Rix and Eric Barham's 28 bhp 803 cc Austin engine of 1952, there developed a great series of small engines.

Prototypes

For a small company, the old Donald Healey Motor Company designed, built and developed a tremendous number of motorcars and boats. In addition to the range of big Healeys and their derivatives, there was a large number of Sprite variants and competition models.

The TFR Targa Florio series, the LM Le Mans series, and the ST Sebring race cars are described in the competition chapters. In addition there were the Sebring and Super Sprites, produced as possible production cars, and a number produced under unlikely code names. Coding started with XI, the original 8 foot short-wheel-base bug that preceeded the Silverstones and reached X400, a prototype 4-litre car. Of course a large number of these were never fully developed. Later we started using code words, such as Daz, Omo, Oxo, Merc, Mars, Eros, Zeus, Scylla, Murgyn, Lion, Ram, Zebra, Python, Bison, Squid, Zulu, Epox, Midas, Iwou, Ajax, Vim, plus a lot of BMC allocated ADO numbers.

The cars built using the washing powder brand names were lightweights. Mars was a development of a MkII Sprite fitted with a 1622 cc MGA engine and gearbox. We started this project in 1961 when we were not happy with the way the Sprite engine was developing as a long stroke 1098 cc unit of dubious strength. To maintain the excellent weight distribution of the Sprite, we took a standard car, cut the front suspension off and pushed it forward 3 inches, extending the front of the chassis to meet it. We used one of the 'A' series 3.73 rear axles and built a one-piece aluminium bonnet on the lines of the

Le Mans 1960: John Dalton and John Colgate drove this special bodied Sprite to a class win. (Edward Eves)

One of two MkI Sprites built specially for rally work at Warwick, on the Alpine Rally driven by journalists Tommy Wisdom and Jack Hay. It finished second overall in the GT category. (Edward Eves)

The cockpit of a prototype steel-bodied version of a coupé Sprite which we tried to put into production. This should be compared with the stark cockpit of the racing version.

Targa Florio cars. We fitted Lockheed disc brakes at the front and the complete car scaled under 15 cwt.

The performance of the car was good but not spectacular, its top speed being 106 mph with a 0–60 mph acceleration time of 9 seconds. As installed, the engine gave 83.5 bhp at 5500 rpm and the car regularly returned 28 to 30 miles per gallon. I did a pretty big mileage in this car. It was extremely noisy – the 1622 engine was a noisy unit and the small Sprite had little in the way of sound deadening. It would obviously have clashed with the MGB and in May 1963 it was sold.

Syd Enever went one better and fitted an MGB engine in a Sprite without increasing the wheelbase. His son, Roger, raced the device. In theory the Sprite axles should have wilted under the torque of these units, but in practice the gears showed no signs of distress. The BMC 'A' series crown wheel and pinion were of course very robust, despite having been originally designed for 803 cc engines.

When the MkII Sprite was in production, its sales together with those of the MkI Midget did not come up to forecasts. It was suggested that this might be because of its price and so in collaboration with BMC we started investigating the possibilities of producing a car at a lower cost. DMH and I drew up a specification for the car and set about building it. A MkI body shell was obtained from BMC's service department and a basic 1098 cc single carburettor engine from Austin production. We designed and built a new one-piece bonnet with lamps in the wings. A panel was cut out of the number plate recess in the tail and the spare wheel was fitted into this, with a locking cover. In the end we had a lighter and better looking car than the MkII. With a lot of detail changes this showed a cost saving which would have meant £75 to the buyer. The whole thing was done very quickly but whilst the project was being debated sales began to improve and the need to reduce the price disappeared.

In March 1964, the MkIII/MkII Spridget was introduced with the new modified rear suspension, incorporating semi-elliptic springs. Whilst the new spring set-up was satisfactory for the production vehicles, it posed some problems for the competition cars. The low weight of the Sprite meant that we had to use low rate springs, and the increased torque of the race engines resulted in the springs winding up on acceleration. We therefore decided to extend the the SM4 development work in the hope of finding a cure.

To cope with axle wind up, we put back one of the torque arms on top of the axle which provided more positive location. However, we found that this system produced judder on acceleration and under severe braking conditions. In addition, we found that we needed new springs after a long race, as they were becoming S-shaped between the axles and the front eye. The front part of the spring, which pushes the cars, was being subjected to increased compression as a result of torque reaction through the torque arm. After some head scratching, we decided that if we put torque reaction members underneath the springs, they would do the pushing and eliminate the deformation of the spring. We therefore deleted the upper torque member and instead fitted one under each spring, as with the American traction master device. During track development, we discovered an added bonus, in that we could now play with the rubbers and setting to obtain a setting that reduced wheel hop under braking. Much of this test work was done with John Moore of Automotive Products, who raced Sprites for Richard Groves.

John had a phobia about twitch, as he had done a lot of his racing on an old and somewhat out of line Sprite, which was very twitchy. Our cars showed a slight semblance of twitch when going over a slight bump on the track. This threw the car slightly off its line, with the result that a certain amount of steering correction was necessary on corners. We eliminated slight discrepancies in the steering and tried bigger rear dampers, with some improvement. At Armstrong's suggestion, we then tried direct acting telescopic dampers, but without any noticeable change. Thinking that we would really tie the rear wheels up, we next fitted both the telescopic dampers and the adjustable lever arm damper. This plan of action, carried out in desperation, completely eliminated any

The Nürburgring: Clive Baker watches John Moore and Richard Groves at work on the ex-works Targa Florio Sprite.

twitchiness. What is more, it meant that we could use a lower total damping force on each wheel than had been possible with just the one damper. Thus, not only had we improved road holding, but with lower settings in the dampers we had eliminated damper fade. Using two dampers per wheel! Maybe Bill Heynes had a similar experience when he fitted four dampers on the independent rear axle of the Jaguar, which gives such a wonderful ride. Anyone contemplating competing with a Sprite should think about adding a pair of telescopic dampers to the rear, as it is a simple operation that really works.

Under our general arrangement with BMC we designed and developed cars more or less as we felt the situation demanded. At times BMC asked us to deal with specific problems or new designs. In this somewhat loose but amicable spirit of co-operation, MG also functioned. In 1965, it occurred to BMC that perhaps there was a need for a more formal approach to the problem of producing a Sprite replacement. Whilst the Sprite and Midget were selling well in a firmly established sector of the market, one always planned to be in a position to introduce something new before sales declined.

At that time BMC were getting excellent results with hydrolastic suspension and it seemed that future suspensions would be based on this system. Sports cars always had to take units stemming from the main mass production lines.

In a meeting at Longbridge, BMC decided that three different designs should be laid down and developed. Austin with their world leadership in transverse-engined front-wheel-drive cars would produce a front-wheel-drive sports car prototype. Syd Enever at MG would produce a Sprite with hydrolastic suspension, and we at Warwick would produce a car with hydrolastic suspension and a 1275 cc transverse engine at the rear. Our project bore the code name WAEC, being the initial letters of 'Wheel At Each Corner'. Geoff Cooper of Austin supplied the drawings of the 1100 suspension and subframes and we laid out a chassis platform to take them. The engine was a 1275 Cooper S. Les Ireland did the body design incorporating some features that DMH wanted. The car was wide, short and low, an open two-seater with a built-in roll over bar of the type later to be referred to as a Targa top. We built in a rear window that could be raised or lowered by a Smith's electric window winder. The hood extended from the screen to the bar and we struggled hard to make it tuck away behind the bar when out of use. We never got this feature to work properly.

In practice the winding rear window worked perfectly, but when it was in the open position the noise from the engine just behind the seats was most objectionable. We used a well raked curved screen, working close to the optical limits decreed by Triplex. From our models, Triplex produced two screens in laminated glass to USA specification, with their usual perfect optical performance. Initially we had cooling problems with the side-mounted Mini radiator, then the fan blew air through it from the engine compartment. Fitting a Sprite fan that sucked cool air from outside cured this problem.

With hydrolastic suspension and 1100 sub frames, the car was heavier than the Sprite which impaired performance. Lockheed produced a set of four wheel disc brakes of a new design, single piston calipers made from steel plate. I had to harry Ron Edwards and John Moore to get these brakes quickly, but when we fitted them they did all that was required and were exceedingly efficient for a low cost design.

Tuning a hydrolastic system is a complex operation. With a lot of fiddling we achieved a very comfortable flat ride. The car tended to oversteer with equal tyre pressure all round but in the end we got it right. The 1100 rack and pinion steering ratio was too low, demanding much wheel twirling when negotiating bends. With a preponderance of weight on the rear wheels and independent hydraulic suspension all round, the road holding was leech-like though one was never sure when the rear end would break away.

This car was considered to be too way out for the sports car market, which is highly conservative, and it would have been expensive to produce. The other two designs at Austin and MG also faded from the scene as it appeared that the Sprite/Midget design, always a good profit earner, had a long life ahead of it.

In the end all these projects were dropped and Syd Enever sent U1, as the car was known, to Triumph who were then in an ascendant position in the

WAEC: the mid-engined prototype with hydrolastic suspension. The flexible roof was being developed to fold into the roll-over bar. The front wheels are different to those at the rear, in order to clear the new front brakes.

Leyland organization. Before it left, I took a series of photographs for the record, but foolishly lent them to someone. Thus not much remains of the project. The gearshift was not really acceptable and would have needed a lot of development. It must be assumed that this car has been scrapped.

On a number of occasions we looked to Coventry Climax as a source of supply for engines. Leonard Lee, the boss of Coventry Climax, was responsible for a tremendous amount of development in the field of engine technology. His company had established world leadership with their lightweight high performance units, while their racing engines enabled British racing car constructors such as Cooper and Lotus to dominate the formula one scene. To the disgust of many people, he never received any acknowledgement or reward for these services from the British Government.

We used the beautiful little 1100 cc single overhead camshaft engine in a car we wanted to market as a Super Sprite. This simple yet efficient engine design had been pioneered by Climax and was later adopted by many major manufacturers like FIAT, Chrysler, Triumph and belatedly Austin-Morris, as the basis for their small car engines. Our project started in 1959 but went on for

XQHS: the original Super Sprite, which was later fitted with a Coventry Climax engine. Les Ireland designed this body, built on standard MkI understructure.

many years. We built three different prototypes in all, producing complete drawings, specifications and costings. However, BMC would never agree to it being put into production and finally squashed the project, telling us not to work with engine manufacturers outside the group.

Later, when Coventry Climax joined Jaguar and then became part of the British Motor Holdings combine together with BMC, we worked with their engine development team again—first on the Healey SR Le Mans car, and then on a $2\frac{1}{2}$ litre sports car with four-speed Jaguar gearbox that would have been a worthy successor to the 3000. However, under the wing of the BMH giant, the Coventry Climax organization was to be deprived of its engine production and design facility and reverted to being a supplier of fork lift trucks. The complete history of Coventry Climax engines has been most expertly told by our old friends, Wally Hassan and Graham Robson. Their book, *Climax in Coventry*, should be on the desk of anyone interested in motors or engines.

Every time we wanted to test a prototype or development car for maximum speed, we used to borrow a surveyor's chain from the county council surveyor and measure and mark a quarter mile. This process is very accurate but it does take time. On one occasion our friends in Coventry decided to speed up the process by making a permanent set of marks. They surveyed a quarter mile and drove in two lengths of steel water pipe at each end, on the grass verge, with about 6 inches sticking out of the ground. This worked beautifully—all we had to do was to drop a wooden rod into each of the pipes and the distance was then clearly marked. Then the local council decided to cut the grass on the verge. The cutter struck the pipes and smashed itself up. Out came the council's maintenance men to fit a new cutter. Exactly 440 yards up the road, this struck the second marker pipe. Naturally, the council were moved to wrath. Soon afterwards, the instigators of the system arrived to test a car. Realizing what had happened, they rang us up to warn us that the road was not usable. I believe they quietly settled the matter with the council. Out testing usually took place at dawn, when there were few people about and when the wind had not got up and the air was cool.

Quite a lot of our development resources were taken up by the need to meet changes, or proposed changes, in the various safety or emission regulations. On a number of occasions, the time scale involved in introducing an alteration to the production cars meant that we built in certain features which proved to be quite unneccessary when the final standards were belatedly issued. One could be forgiven for thinking that the British and American automobile industries deliberately make their cars unsafe, if one listened to all the outpourings of the critics. Nothing could be further from the truth. Our primary interest was to sell motor cars, and unsafe cars do not sell well. An engineer's training emphasizes the need to avoid failures through design and development, with particular emphasis being placed on those areas where failure could cause accidents.

We always designed components and assemblies with fail-safe features. Bolts were fitted so that if they came loose they could not fall out, or if they did come out they could not jam a vital part. In the old days bolts and nuts were locked with cotter pins, locking wire or tab washers. Today's locking nuts are much more reliable and modern thread locking compounds like Loctite are even more effective, the only problem being that it is not possible to see that the thread has been locked.

Hastily introduced safety measures often resulted in the introduction of added hazards. The early steering column locks could very occasionally lock the column before the key was removed. We had to fit a safety plate to a batch of column locks on Spridgets to prevent the locking pawl dropping into the locked position when the car was being driven. These plates rendered the locking mechanism ineffective but left the anti-theft properties of the precision key and barrel unaffected. In theory this was a temporary measure until an improved and fault-free lock could be introduced, but most owners did not bother to bring their cars in for the change. The large number of key combinations required and the high precision necessary to obtain this, resulted in locks jamming due to debris picked up by the key in the owner's pocket getting into the barrel. The irate owner would then be stranded with a car which could not be started until the lock was cut off with a hacksaw and a replacement fitted.

The controlled collapse built into the front and rear ends of the car's body was effective in reducing injuries to vehicle occupants, though a number of rally drivers found that the extreme stress and strain of rallying resulted in body failure in these areas. Not all safety column designs were reliable, some starting to collapse under normal driving conditions. Massive safety bumpers, such as those on the current Midget, were designed to reduce damage to cars in low speed collisions and thereby reduce repair costs. In fact, they have resulted in an overall increase in motoring costs, adding considerably to the cost of the vehicle and increasing repair costs in most accidents to undesirably high figures.

After the Second World War, we changed over to a unified system of screw threads, fixings, nuts and bolts that was compatible with the Society of Automotive Engineers' standards of use in the USA. This change, a wise one, cost a lot of money but it did bring a degree of standardization to the industry and resulting benefits to the customer. Now our dreamers are forcing the diabolical metric system upon us, with its much inferior and less safe system of screw threads. The Big Healeys and the Spridgets were built using unified SAE standards, while the Jensen Healey was laid down to conform to metric standards.

The officials who think up safety and emission laws and other such regulations appear to have no idea of the costs involved, or of the time needed to introduce the systems required on production vehicles. The costs of meeting these standards has risen dramatically over the years, and it is the motoring public that finally pays the bill.

The Targa Florio

One of the world's oldest motor races began in Sicily. Count Vincenzo Florio organized the first Targa Florio in 1906, as a real road race over the 45-mile Piccolo Circuito delle Madonie. Over the years, the actual circuit has varied, but in the 1960s the course was very similar to the original, with tarmac replacing the dirt surface of long ago. The roads are repaired before the race, but some seventy odd sports cars very quickly remove the patching to produce even bigger potholes than before. Various estimates of the number of corners have been made–Tommy Wisdom used to say that there were 700–but in fact the course is virtually all corners, with one poor straight of about 4 miles along the northern coast from Campofelice to within 2 miles of the finish. The start and finish are.at Cerda, with its concrete tribunes and pits. The race covers ten laps, and is a real test of every part of a car.

The first time a Healey car entered the Targa Florio was in 1948, when a works 2.4-litre saloon driven by Johnny Lurani and Dorino Serafini finished thirteenth overall and first in the unlimited touring car category. In 1949, Tommy Wisdom and Tony Hume drove a works Silverstone to sixteenth position, coming fourth in the class. In both years the cars were the first British finishers.

In 1959, Tommy Wisdom approached us with a scheme to run a Sprite with Bernard Cahier. Tommy and DMH got Austin's approval and we prepared a Frog-eye, under our code number TFR1. The engine power was increased by fitting a sports camshaft, polishing the ports and fitting two larger $1\frac{1}{2}$ inch

Tommy Wisdom and Douglas Johns in the 1959 Monte Carlo Rally. Note that the standard grille has been opened up for extra cooling. (Edward Eves)

SU carburettors. To improve the braking the larger 8 inch Austin A40 brakes and drums were fitted to the front while Mintex supplied shoes lined with their reliable old M20 material. Every part of the car was checked over and some nuts and bolts that might have worked loose were wire locked.

Tommy drove the car from Warwick to Italy, picking up Bernard Cahier en route. Margot and I flew to Palermo by BEA Viscount and Alitalia Dakota (DC 3), where we picked up a Hertz 1100 Fiat. We were based in the Jolly Hotel in Palermo and I did all the preparation work in the hotel's basement garage. Knowing that foreign oil is often suspect, I emptied the Italian Shell tins and refilled them with British Castrol R40. The drivers were contracted to Shell but we were using Castrol at that time. Margot dealt with the formalities of scrutineering and feeding.

Most of the drivers used Hertz rental Fiats to learn the course, which meant that there was a lot of competition between teams to get hold of the quickest available. Drivers do not take it easy when learning a circuit, and the rental cars were not usually in the best condition when returned to Hertz. Tommy Wisdom took Margot and me on one of his learning runs, which proved most valuable in developing the Sprite.

Although Tommy knew the circuit pretty well, he always maintained that there was a constant danger of mistaking a fast bend for a slow one. He concentrated on learning the difficult corners, some of which were identified by post markings made by rally drivers. He could identify most stretches of the road with some incident in previous races. Very few drivers ever learnt the circuit well enough to be able to drive near the limit, though the spectacular local ace Nino Vaccarella was possibly an exception to this rule.

Tommy and Bernard did one lap each in official practice and were reasonably happy, wanting only minimal alterations. In the race, they were to drive alternately, taking two laps at a time. Two laps of the long 45-mile circuit was not going to leave much reserve from the 5-gallon petrol tank, so they obtained a 5-litre plastic petrol can which was stowed behind the seat.

Well before dawn on the day of the race, we travelled out to the start at Cerda. The cars started at intervals, the smallest first. I saw Tommy away to a good start. Some fifty minutes later an irate and uncomfortable Wisdom pulled into the pits. The plastic can had burst, dousing the driver's seat with petrol. Someone threw a bucket of water in the car to wash out the remains and mopped it up, while Tommy somehow washed himself down. After topping up with petrol, Bernard set off for the next two laps. Despite the delay the car was running well and in a good position.

Just when we looked like doing really well, with Tommy on his last lap, the throttle cable broke. To Tommy, with his vast experience, this was not a great problem. He wired the throttle open and completed the race using the ignition switch to shut the engine on and off, which is not an easy matter on such a demanding circuit. His final place, seventeenth overall and sixth in class, was not bad but nevertheless disappointing.

Back at Warwick we looked at the throttle cable. Whilst the production cable had a good record in normal service we needed something stronger for racing. Roger Menadue went to the local cycle shop and came back with a motor cycle clutch cable assembly of appropriate length. We were to use these cables on all later racing Sprites without one failure.

This same car was much more highly modified for 1960, when Stirling Moss took it to second place in the Sebring Four Hour race. In June 1960 it was driven in the Alpine Rally by Tommy Wisdom and Jack Hay with a specially built 995 cc engine and a Shorrock supercharger, but it did not complete the course. It was badly damaged on the return journey and was sold in September 1960.

We did not go to the Targa Florio again until 1964. Tommy Wisdom organized additional funds once more and we built TFR2, a lightweight

The 1964 Targa Florio Sprite, showing the raised tail and spoiler.

open two-seater. This was the first of the very special Targa Florio cars, and was also the first Sprite to be fitted with half elliptic rear springs. On to the standard Sprite understructure, we fitted a Birmabright light alloy body, hand formed by Bill Buckingham and Terry Westwood in our experimental bodyshop. We built a larger fuel tank to ensure that the car would be capable of covering three laps without refuelling, and fitted a laminated Mini windscreen. I tested the car around the Warwickshire roads, having first equipped it with an extra silencer to quieten down the open racing exhaust system.

Margot and I decided to take the car down to Sicily, fitting a large luggage rack and loading it up with my tool kit and spares for the race. Dunlop arranged to transport the spare wheels and tyres direct to Palermo. We took the ferry from Dover to Ostend and then loaded the car onto the night train to Milan. This Victorian method of travel is pleasant and also saved wearing out the car on the most tiresome part of the journey. Our only problem was in trying to avoid overheating in the Naples traffic! Margot used all her knowledge of Italian ways to get the car loaded into one of the few places below decks on the Naples-Palermo ferry, much to the annoyance of the Lancia team.

In Palermo we met up with Derek Blunsden, a mining engineer resident in Sicily who was always most helpful during our Targa Florio expeditions. Tommy Wisdom and Paddy Hopkirk arrived that evening, and we were also joined by Stuart Turner, who wanted to find out if the Targa would suit BMC's Competitions Department's future programme.

In practice, the special petrol tank built at Warwick developed a leak on the bottom seam, which meant that I had a struggle in a hot Palermo garage, getting it out and soldering it up with the aid of the proprietor. This garage was full of FIATs in bits, the result of enthusiastic Italians overdoing it on the circuit. The highlight was a works gull wing Mercedes belonging to a well

The 1964 Targa Florio was later fitted with a short hard top extending just beyond the louvres. This was extended to the tail by Richard Groves when he took the car over in 1965.

known German racing driver, hidden away in one corner.

In the race, Paddy broke a half shaft during his first stint, which put him out of the running. BMC had recently commonized the axle shaft specification for all the 'A' series axles, using a lower grade material than on the earlier cars. This failure highlighted the weakness, and we were able to get the shafts changed before they went into the production Sprites.

TFR2 had shown a strong tendency to understeer, an unwelcome feature on the Targa Florio's twisty circuit. For 1965 we built another special, TFR3, which incorporated some subtle changes in the body design. The fuel tank was moved further back and lower down, and the inclination of the rear springs was reduced, lessening the effects of roll understeer. These modifications were sufficient to turn the car into the perfect candidate for the Targa's Circuito Piccolo delle Madonie – quick to turn into a corner, while giving good traction on the exit. In fact, I still consider TFR3 to be the best and most lovable of all the special Sprites. We painted it with a light green paint, Dockers Docka-colour, which stood out well in the sunlight.

I learnt from one of the press men that Castrol were taking a special interest in the 1965 event, and intended to make a special film. I immediately rang Stuart Turner and asked him to confirm the truth of these rumours. He agreed

1965 Targa Florio: Rauno Aaltonen about to set off on a practice lap, with a Ford GT40 next in line.

The 1965 Targa Florio car, a very practical and lovable road car. The circular object at the rear of the front wing is the breather from the engine oil tank. The roll cage and Dunlop bonded windscreen added greatly to the rigidity of the structure.

with me that this gave us the chance for some real publicity – a commodity he always appreciated – and decided to enter a 3000 and one of the GT Midgets.

As before, Margot and I loaded up the car with spares and set off from Warwick. We met up with the Abingdon contingent at Dover and then continued in convoy. We were all driving down the Autostrada del Sole, at a moderate speed in steady drizzle, when we rounded a bend to find the road obstructed by an accident. We stopped easily, as did Clive Baker who was following us, but poor Nobby Clarke in the Midget was not so lucky. His cold, wet disc brakes failed to respond instantly and he nudged a policeman who was running up the road to warn cars of the incident. The policeman did a good imitation of a professional footballer trying to win a penalty by lying on the ground and groaning. We looked like being in real trouble as the policeman's superior, who was at the scene of the accident, was not at all friendly. It seemed as though we were in for a long delay and that Nobby might have to go to gaol. However, then a very senior policeman arrived. Margot had a long conversation with him and they were soon both laughing and joking. At length, he delivered his judgement: the policeman who caused the incident had been stupid to run up the road, but Nobby must have been going too fast for the conditions. A payment of 10,000 lire would be appropriate and would cover the cleaning of the policeman's uniform, and would we please proceed more sedately, reserving the racing for Sicily. The victim instantly recovered and shook hands and we set off with a receipt for the fine. We could not now make Naples that night so Margot suggested we stopped at Frascati. Entering the town we spotted 'Hotel Eden' where we had an excellent meal, washed down with some superb local Frascati produced from the vineyards of the proprietor. We all slept well in comfortable beds which could so easily have been bunks in a cell!

The next night was spent on the ferry from Naples to Palermo. The team was based at the Lido at Trabia, not far from the start and on the very edge of the sea. We started the day with a dip in the Mediterranean, then free of pollution at Trabia, followed by breakfast. Scrutineering took place at the tribunes or pits, where the officials were very helpful and tolerant. Practice went well, the Sprite being one of the ten quickest cars. The 3000 was undertyred for this type of race and its tyres would have to be changed at least twice. After practice we always made a work list for each of the cars, noting all the changes the drivers wanted, as well as routine changes of engine oil and filter. After a pretty swift lap by Rauno Aaltonen, I duly filled out the list including the note 'remove power restrictors' and stuck it to the windscreen. Alec Poole, who always took a keen interest in everything, read it and called over his partner Andrew Hedges. They then buttonholed Rauno and Clive and queried the power restrictors and why we used them. Rauno told them that it was to save the car for the race and mislead the opposition.

The principle tuning of the Sprite for the Targa Florio was adjusting the engine tie rod and level of petrol in the Weber carburettor. This setting was critical as flooding caused the engine to blubber out of the corners, while too low a level caused it to cut momentarily. It was a simple matter to get it just right on a convenient piece of road outside the hotel.

We spent some time with Tommy Wisdom and the Castrol men who were making the film. Timo took the cameraman for a circuit of the course in the spare Healey. The film team did a magnificent job and the film, 'Mountain Legend', is a classic, capturing the atmosphere of the Targa Florio completely. In its bright green paint the Sprite really stands out.

With packed lunches we set off early for the pits. Crowds build up early as the Sicilians rush out to vantage points round the course. Stuart Turner was of course in charge of everything, a function he performed with the least formality and the greatest efficiency. Keeping a mixture of amateur, professional racing and rally drivers in line is not an easy task. Our Sprite was to be driven by Rauno Aaltonen and Clive Baker. We were supported by John Harris who flew in to act as mechanic, together with brother Brian and our old friend Derek Blunsden.

The plan was for Rauno to do three laps, Clive four if we felt the fuel consumption allowed, and then Rauno the final three. He set off at a cracking pace but came in at the end of his stint complaining that the left front brake was locking. John and I quickly had the wheel off and found that the brake was binding as the pistons would not retract. We could not lever them back without using a great deal of force. We checked pedal free play and it became apparent that the pistons were seizing in the calipers. This stop cost us 15 minutes of intensive work and even then the brakes were not completely free from grabbing. Clive and Rauno took the car to fifteenth position and second in class. One of our best chances of a win had been wasted.

The cause of the trouble was apparently a build up of manufacturing tolerances in the Lockheed caliper. John Moore of Lockheed was able to increase clearances on later calipers which overcame the problem and increased pad life.

All three of our cars finished with a second position in their respective classes and a great deal of publicity. However, the undisputed highlight of the racing was the driving of Nino Vaccarella in a Ferrari. A local hero, Vaccarella's approach was heralded by cheers from the crowd as he and Bandini forced the Ferrari to first place, knocking 40 seconds off the lap record to

The 1965 Targa Florio. Left to right: Rauno Aaltonen, Clive (Nurgler) Baker, Tommy Wisdom and GCH.

finish over four minutes ahead of Colin Davis in the leading Porsche. The Targa Florio was always a great contest between Ferrari and Porsche.

TFR3 was used as a road car after the race, equipped with a spark plug provided by Laurie Hands of Champion. I drove it down to Cornwall on many occasions, on fishing trips with my old friend Trevor Vage, and it became one of my favourite cars of all times. It rarely oiled a plug, provided the correct starting procedure was observed. Running a car on the road as much as possible, and lending it to friends, often led to valuable improvements as a result of one's own experience or the comments, rude or otherwise, of others.

For 1966 we converted TFR3 into the TFR4 coupé. This was a relatively simple operation. We formed an aluminium top with a perspex rear window and two side windows, adding drop perspex windows in the doors, with external push buttons to operate the locks. Rauno Aaltonen was the prime mover in this conversion, maintaining that a roof would provide greater protection in the event of an accident on the Targa's somewhat hair-raising course. I always thought that an open car should be quicker on this particular circuit.

The 1966 event was the 50th Targa Florio, and the program included some of the vintage cars that had competed many years before, their commemmorative runs contrasting sharply with the performance put up by the current entries. Rauno Aaltonen and Clive Baker, our team of one rally and one racing driver,

The 1966 Targa Florio Sprite: this was the 1965 car with a light alloy top built on.

The MG and Healey team queue for the ferry at Palermo after the Targa Florio.

again took the wheel of the Sprite.

Rain, an unusual occurrence in Sicily at that time of the year, made the track wet. This should have helped the Sprite's chances but any benefit was unfortunately soon cancelled out. Rauno slid back against some rock and knocked a 3 by 1 inch piece out of the wheel rim, also knocking the rear axle slightly askew. We hurriedly fitted a new wheel and tyre, refuelled the car and sent it away with Clive at the wheel. He failed to appear on time at the end of his first lap. The half shaft had broken, which Clive claimed to have replaced single-handed. Later we learnt that a couple of English enthusiasts had leapt to help when they spotted Clive at work. We always carried a spare half shaft in the race cars after the 1964 incident! Despite loss of time, we finished sixteenth overall and third in class.

For 1967 we built a new car, TFR5. This incorporated many improvements, including Girling light alloy caliper disc brakes all round, reduced windscreen and doubled up rear dampers. Clive was again to suffer misfortune. Approaching a bend, he braked hard just as a local decided to run across the road. The man ended up across the windscreen and Clive hit the guard-rails, knocking the front end askew. The local police locked Clive up, mainly in case any of the locals sought revenge and later delivered him by helicopter to the pits. After the race an enthusiastic helper, Margot and I recovered the car with the barge and towed it in, arriving back at Trabia just as Stuart and the drivers were departing for the official reception at the Palace in Palermo. Unfortunately we were tired and filthy and unable to make the party. Despite the

The 1293 cc Sprite of Clive Baker and Rauno Aaltonen at speed in the 1967 Targa Florio, before the accident caused by a spectator who ran across the road.

Jack Wheeler in his privately entered Sprite in the 1967 Targa Florio. After a lot of troubles, it finished sixth in the class.

The 1967 Targa Florio. Despite the heavy roll bar, the car is over at quite an angle.

Sicilians' reputation for banditry, the car was complete. In fact, the Sicilians have a proper respect for racing cars.

1968 saw TFR6 running in the sports car class. This Sprite was a highly modified production-bodied Mk IV, with a 1293 cc dry sump engine, 5 speed box and Minilite centre lock wheels. The car went very quickly and should have won the class but it suddenly boiled and lost water. Clive kept going in an attempt to reach the pits, completely wrecking the engine in the process. The car was then rebuilt and subsequently entered by Clive Baker and Andrew Hedges in the Mugello sports car race held in the Appenines just outside Florence. This race was very popular with private entrants, being a great deal

The last racing Sprite built at Warwick: wedge-shaped and light, with a Lucas petrol-injected 1293 engine, four-wheel Girling racing disc brakes and panelled by Bill Bucking-ham in Birmabright high strength aluminium alloy. This looked so good that we never painted it. The car was sold to Ed Bussey of West Palm Beach.

more accessible than the Targo Florio and run over a course that was generally considered to be a lot easier, though of similar length. Clive and Andrew took the car to fifteenth position overall, with first place in class.

The last of the TFR series, TFR7, was built for the 1969 Targa Florio, incorporating all the knowledge we had gained on our previous six sorties with Sprites. We started with the basic understructure from John Thompson's of Wolverhampton, from which we cut away all the unwanted pieces like the wheel arches and the flat steel panels, replacing them with hard Birmabright sheet. We removed the gearbox tunnel and substituted a larger tunnel fabricated in 20 gauge sheet steel to take the special 5 speed gearbox. Chassis extensions from the rear of the platform were needed to carry the petrol tank and rear

spring hangers. These we fabricated and assembled in the crude jig we had made, welding or brazing them with Eutectic 16, a very strong low temperature rod.

Barry Bilbie and I had drawn up the abbreviated body to comply with the basic FIA prototype sports car regulations, basing the design on the Le Mans coupés without windscreen and top. We added a simple rear end, designed to provide some downward force. The wooden buck on which the Le Mans bodies were built was quickly modified and Bill Buckingham and Terry Westwood set to, producing the body in 20 gauge half hard Birmabright sheet. The completed body looked so impressive that we decided not to spoil it with paint. The excellent corrosion resistance of Birmabright made any protection unnecessary.

The power unit was the last of the Le Mans units. Not many people realized the very special nature of these since we deliberately kept quiet about any developments, the aim of competition being to boost sales to the standard product. The units were based on the 1275 cc Sprite engine with the bore increased by 20 thou or half a millimetre to 71.12 mm. With a stroke of 81.28 mm this gave a capacity of 1293 cc. The blocks were specially cast with a very thick central main bearing web and were fitted with SG iron main bearing caps. A special light alloy sump or oil pan replaced the pressed steel unit and added to the rigidity of the whole unit. The crankshaft of special steel was nitride hardened and fitted with a proper oil seal at the rear.

The heads were new castings, with four inlet ports and sparking plugs on the right-hand side and four exhaust ports on the left. In addition the head castings were Tuftrided, a process that reduced the unduly high incidence of heads cracking between the valve seats. The heads had very small combustion chambers with a resultant compression ratio of 12.5 to 1.

The fuel supply was from a rear mounted tank incorporating a very effective catch pit to Lucas's recommendations. A Lucas fuel pump supplied fuel at 120 psi to the metering pump which was driven by a cogged belt from the crankshaft. The fuel injection nozzles were located upstream in the cast aluminium trumpets with the throttle opening controlled by SU butterflies. The Lucas injection system was very reliable, very effective and surprisingly economical. The throttle response was instantaneous and there were none of the problems with fuel surge on cornering and braking that carburettor units normally give under high G forces. The engines used a dry sump oil system carrying two gallons of Castrol R 30 in a light alloy tank in the passenger's foot well. For these tanks we sought the advice of Wally Hassan of Coventry Climax. As usual he gave us the right information and the air was effectively separated from the oil.

Like the engine, the gearbox was developed by Eddie Maher and his team at Morris Motors' engine branch at Coventry. It was based on the gears used in the MGB, in a special casing with the fifth speed in a compartment behind the main box. These boxes were strong, reliable and a joy to use.

The front suspension followed the basic Sprite pattern, with one of the heavier 3000 antiroll bars. The rear suspension used special Bramber half elliptic leaf springs with adjustable torque reaction rods. Four dampers were fitted at the rear – a pair of adjustable lever arm DAS 10 Armstrongs and a supplementary pair of telescopic units. The perennial problem of damper fade was finally overcome with this set-up, where the dampers were only lightly stressed.

Sadly, this car was never raced by us, although it was ready to run in the 1969 Targa Florio. British Leyland's recent clampdown on competition meant that they would not have given us any support, financial or otherwise, for our entry. Additionally, we knew by then that the Sprite was to drop out of production at the end of the year, and so there seemed little point in going racing with a Sprite. A couple of very good Italian drivers asked us if they could borrow the car for the race but we decided against it, and instead sold it to our friend, Ed Bussey, the MG and Austin distributor in Florida. I was particularly

Simple instrumentation on a light racing car.

disappointed at missing the race: TFR7 had benefited from the most extensive development of all the TFR cars, and certainly promised to have been ideal for the Targa's circuit.

The Targa Florio no longer forms part of the international racing calendar. Despite an exceptionally good safety record, with low average speeds imposed by the numerous bends of the circuit and only one fatality in over 60 years, serious accidents in less arduous races and the introduction of various safety regulations have deprived it of its international status. However, it is still run as a national event for Italian drivers—and Italian drivers having a go provide a spectacle not quickly forgotten. We always considered the Circuito Piccolo delle Madonie an ideal development ground, and a lot of what we learnt was incorporated in subsequent production models.

Sebring, Sunshine and Sprites

I first visited the USA with DMH in February 1948, taking along a 2.4 litre Riley engined Healey Roadster. We took our driving tests in New York and then embarked on a long cross country trip down to Los Angeles, supplied with maps and routes by the ever helpful American Automobile Association. The AAA made one slight mistake, directing us over the summer scenic route to the north. We struggled over the mountains with the SU carburettors freezing up at frequent intervals until we built a shield and got a hot air supply to them. Otherwise the car was absolutely trouble free, apart from a tendency to collecting speeding tickets. This first trip was an educational experience of great importance. It really gave us an insight into American motoring conditions and helped us form ideas of what type of car was needed for this hugely important export market.

In the early days I had not been exactly fond of Americans. An American unit was billeted in my home town during the war, and whenever I came back on leave my parents' house and garden seemed to be full of American servicemen from next door. With three sons in the services, my parents appreciated what home comforts meant to a man overseas but to me, being young, it seemed as if these Yanks had usurped my home and comforts. Later, when serving alongside them, I was to learn to appreciate their qualities and way of life.

In 1949 the only British sports car being exported seriously to the USA was the MG TC Midget. In the purists' eyes, this was the only true Midget, being a thoroughbred MG design stemming from their prewar series, with open

Dad's army on leave! Ivy, John, GCH, Brian and DMH.

two-seater traditional bodywork and separate headlamps, the wings flaring out from the body. Even so, this car was slower than nearly all the American production cars of the period. The sales and service network for British cars was then pretty thin on the ground, though of course this was less than three years after the war from which we were still recovering. All the dealers we met were crying out for suitable sports cars. The Healey Roadster was far too expensive and not really sporting enough, but the contacts we made then were to stand us in good stead when we started exporting the Austin Healey 100.

In 1953, during a sales tour of America, DMH took one of the first 100s to Sebring. His intention was not to compete, but just to have a look at the race and see what it was all about. Alec Ullman had taken over the disused Hendricks airfield as part of his business operations in aircraft. Being a great sportsman and enthusiast, he had also started to organize a great series of races on this cunningly converted airfield circuit. With Mary Ullman, Fred Royston, Reg Smith, Monty Thomas and many others, Alec was to raise one such event, the 12-hour race, to world championship status, to rank with the very much older Targa Florio, Le Mans 24 Hours and Nürburgring 1000 Km as a classic long distance event. The courtesy and help this dedicated band of enthusiasts extended to competitors was wonderful, especially as most were continually trying to bend the regulations to their advantage. Over the years, chief scrutineer Monty Thomas and his assistant Elmer Dew were to put all the cars through rigorous examinations with friendly efficiency, showing no bias towards either the most prestigious teams or the poorest. Certainly, no favours were ever shown to US nationals. With its vast crowds of enthusiasts and excellent press coverage, Sebring became the American shop window. It also happened at the right time when the sports car selling season was about to open up. It was very important to us as part of our US promotion and was also popular, as we usually left a rotten British winter for Florida's superb climate and friendly inhabitants.

Shortly after the announcement of the Sprite we decided to enter a team at Sebring in March 1959. This decision was hammered out at a competitions meeting at the Motor Show in October 1958, when all the American and British representatives were assembled, including Ted Birt of Hambro, and Lester Suffiield and Rod Leroyd of the US division of BMC. Outspoken Lester was keen that MG should take complete control of the teams and pits to scotch the infighting that was developing between rival factions in the USA. His wishes were respected and a system was developed whereby BMC's competitions manager had complete control of the team and time-keeping, leaving me free to do the best possible with the Sprites. This system worked perfectly and happily for a number of years.

I had charge of the preparation of the cars down at Warwick and drew up a specification, number ST200. We built four basically standard Sprites with hard tops provided by Jensen. Hambro, the importing organization, would provide the bulk of the helpers, organize accommodation and select the drivers. Our racing budget could not extend to shipping a full team of drivers and in any case it was felt that greater kudos would result if these were North Americans. The drivers selected were Hugh Sutherland/Phil Stiles, Ed Leavens/Dr Kunz/John Colgate, and Fred Hayes/John Christy.

Eddie Maher built the engines at Coventry. These were only moderately tuned to 57 bhp with the emphasis being on strength and reliability. Sebring was a tough race being hard on brakes and transmissions. We fitted the then optional disc brakes, that is optional on the homologation form I had compiled but really only available for works cars. These Dunlop brakes, known as 'the light car brake', were light and reliable, a typical example of the Dunlop engineers' ability. Fitted on the Sprite, they would last a full twelve hours without a pad change being necessary. Dunlop also supplied the tyres and the wire wheels. The tyres were of their famed 'Road Speed' type, with excellent

One of the 1959 Sebring 12 hour race Sprites on display at Ed Bussey's West Palm Beach showroom – after the race but still looking like new.

wearing qualities but not especially renowned for their wet road holding. The cars had a top speed of about 98 mph. The special stub axles were made to an improved pattern about to be introduced on production. We had them crack tested, a standard routine with all critical suspension parts, but I can not recall ever finding a crack in any part made by BMC.

These Sebring Sprites were delightful little cars, being very lively and quick for their day. As usual I took the first built down to Cornwall and back for a 500-mile shakedown test.

In the race we were after the class positions and were fortunate to finish first, second and third in class, with the highest placed car driven by Hugh Sunderland and Phil Stiles finishing fifteenth overall in front of some much more powerful entries. The only trouble was in the gearbox of the third car, where the second speed broke. Motoring journalist John Christy was blamed by the ignorant for this, but the Sprite gearbox was its Achilles heel, liable to fail at any time.

As usual Ed Bussey, the Florida distributor, entertained us all after the event with a party at Palm Beach. After the race the cars were sold to any distributor who had a use for them. A car that had taken a hammering for twelve hours on Sebring's arduous circuit needed quite a bit of work to restore it to A1 condition. Ed, of course, bought one and we sent him the bits to put it right.

These three class places, and the resultant publicity, were a good result for all concerned, with supplies of the car just beginning to reach America. I was particularly happy as this killed off a suggestion that had been more than a rumour that all competition work would be transferred to the BMC Competitions Department at Abingdon, on the grounds that they could do it better. There was a lunatic fringe at MG who resented our activities.

For 1960, the organizers of Sebring introduced a four hour race for the smaller cars. This was one we could win. As the race was for GT cars, we could make only minimal alterations, using homologated equipment. We decided to enter TFR1, our first Targa Florio Sprite. The engine was sent to Harry Weslake at Rye for him to try to get just a little bit more power, which of course he did. To make our chances of a win more certain it was decided that we would try to get Stirling Moss to drive it. People always argue as to who is the world's best driver and at that time there were two contenders for that position– Stirling Moss and Juan Fangio. Having known Stirling as a driver of our cars, I will always consider him to be the best. The main opposition to the Sprite in the four-hour race would be the twin cam Abarth cars, whose advanced engines were capable of giving considerably more power. Carlo Abarth was a very clever engineer and had been producing racing cars in Italy for a long time with great success. We knew that our hope for a win lay in Stirling being seconds quicker than almost any other driver.

However, when the car was being driven around prior to the race, it lost water and overheated. On stripping we found that a flaw in the head casting had developed into a hole. Our alternatives were to weld the port at a point about 2 inches in from the manifold, or to fit a production head and lose power. We decided on the former and found a repair shop in Avon Park where the owner, expressing misgivings, welded the head. One inlet port now had a large bump of weld and we did not risk filing much off it. When rebuilt the car seemed to run as well as ever, but it must have lost something at the top end.

The GT restrictions did not apply to the twelve hour race and for this we entered a special Sprite, fitted with a Falcon fibreglass body built by Roger Menadue at Warwick. This was considerably lighter than the production car and was equipped with the Dunlop Light Car disc brakes on all four wheels.

Stirling was to drive a Maserati in the twelve hour race and when he came to try the Sprite he could not start it. Being used to the Maserati central acceleration pedal position, he had instinctively placed his right foot on the

Sprite's central brake pedal. In four quick practice laps Stirling established the speed he could lap at in the race and was able to tell us of a few minor alterations that he required. What was most disconcerting was the speed at which Stirling was wearing the tyres. Previously a Sprite had always done four hours with plenty of tread remaining. The way he was driving we would need a tyre change in under three hours!

During the twelve hour practice Stirling came over and said he would like to try the twelve hour car. Our driver, John Sprinzel, was rated as one of the fastest Sprite drivers and had been going well although he had difficulty in keeping the revs below the stipulated 6500. Stirling did three rapid laps, the quickest being a full four seconds quicker than John's best, while the maximum engine revolutions shown were a few hundred below the stipulated maximum. Stirling was able to tell John where he was loosing time on a couple of bends.

At the start of the four hour race, Dunlop's technical representative suggested that we should use the twelve hour tyres as they might last the four hours; but, of course, these were back at the garage. Stirling made one of his normal good starts but the two fastest Abarths got ahead of him. He took the lead when the Abarths pitted for fuel, but after two and three-quarter hours he had to come in for both tyres and fuel. This lost him a good two minutes to the Abarths who did not need a tyre change. He had to make a second stop for fuel and finished a very close second. We were all a little disappointed with the result when we had been so near to winning.

In the twelve-hour race all went well at the start, but then the car fell back with a blown cylinder head gasket. This was replaced and the drivers struggled on to win the class. Cylinder head gaskets were always a problem on the early Sprites, one that was not really overcome until the cylinder head casting was modified to increase the metal thickness of the joint face. This twelve hour Sprite was used later on that year at Le Mans, where John Colgate and John Dalton drove it to first place in class.

The majority of the mechanics for Sebring came from BMC's US and Canadian operations. Eric Vale, an old Austin man who has just completed fifty years' service, used to drive an Austin truck down from Toronto, laden with spares and equipment. Other mechanics flew down from New York. Most of them were field men, taking the opportunity to work on something that would reach production later. From Abingdon came one or two mechanics like Dougie Watts, Denny Green or Tommy Wellman, and invariably Roger Menadue from Warwick. We relied on the American contingent to bring the tools.

The 1961 Sebring event was a big effort, with ten cars coming from England – two twin cam MGAs plus one practice car and two of our Sprites for the twelve hour race, and three of our Sprites for the four hour race. In addition John Sprinzel produced two of his Sebring Sprites to run in both events. The

The 1961 Sebring team with some of the cars at Avon Park. Back row: Peter Millard, unknown, John Sprinzel, GCH, unknown, Rod Learoyd, Paddy Hopkirk, Brian Griffin, Stan Nichols, Alec Murray, Eric Vale. Front row: Paul Hawkins, unknown, Roger Menadue, unknown, Jack Flaherty, John Whitmore, Dougie Watts, Peter Riley, How Wallace.

whole operation was masterminded by Marcus Chambers who was not altogether happy about the number of Sprites running.

The four-hour line up was impressive, with Walt Hansgen, Bruce McLaren, Briggs Cunningham and Ed Leavens on the Warwick-built Sprites, and Stirling Moss and Pat Moss on John Sprinzel's, with Paul Hawkins as reserve driver. Our Sprites were lightweights with all-fibreglass bodies moulded from a production Frog-Eye. Again we failed to win, being beaten by two very fast and well driven Abarths. Walt Hansgen came third, Bruce McLaren fourth, Stirling Moss fifth, Ed Leavens sixth, Pat Moss and Paul Hawkins seventh and Briggs Cunningham eighth. To ease administration, our team was run by Louis Comito and he arranged a great deal of publicity for us, while Champion gave the very standard-looking Sprites a great build-up.

In the twelve-hour race, Joe Buzetta and Glen Carlson, both Americans, finished fifteenth overall and second in class in one of the Warwick-built

Sebring 1961: Pat Moss, John Sprinzel, Cyril Simpson, Stirling Moss and Bruce McLaren. Stirling is telling John how to get round more quickly.

The Sebring 4 hour race, 1961: Stirling Moss leads Bruce McLaren through a first bend. The tyres imbedded as markers were a dangerous form of edging. (Daniel Rubin)

Sebring 1961: an Abarth followed by Sprinzel's Sprite and a works Sprite. Old US Airforce planes were parked all over the place.

Sprites, while Ed Leavens and John Colgate came twenty-fifth and John Sprinzel and Paul Hawkins thirty-seventh. A shortage of runners in the 1150 cc class had meant that it was combined with the Sprites' 1000 cc class, and the overall class winner was a Lola Climax. The MGA twin cams finished first and second in their class. A one hundred per cent finish with good placings was better than had been anticipated.

For 1962 we constructed four MkII bodies with light alloy panels powered by 998 cc engines for the four hour race. We also entered one 1098 cc coupé, fitted with a special light alloy body built at Warwick, in the 12 hour race. Out of a field of twenty-nine starters in the four hour race, thirteen were Abarths and ten were Sprites. Our cars were driven by Stirling Moss, Pedro Rodriguez, Innes Ireland and actor Steve McQueen. We thought we had it right this time, especially when Stirling pulled out a 9 second lead on the first lap. He held this for the whole of the first forty laps but was then overtaken

Sebring 1962: Stirling Moss making his usual perfect start to gain a 9 second lead on the rest of the field. After the track had dried out, the more powerful Abarth coupés were able to overtake the Sprite near the end of the race.

A night stop at Sebring. Roger Menadue fixes a damaged lamp. The drivers confer and we wait patiently. (Daniel Rubin)

Four Sprites line up for the 3 hour GT Race. Stirling had the bonnet straps changed on his car as he thought this arrangement would save time at a pit stop.

Sebring 1962: 'Have we got Dunlop's latest wet weather compound?' Stirling asks. 'Um – no – Dunlop only have green spots for this size.' Wet weather threatened at the start and if it had continued throughout the race, Stirling would have won easily.

when he came in for fuel with fifteen minutes to go. Bruce McLaren won in an Abarth, while Walt Hansgen was second, Stirling third, Pedro Rodriguez sixth, Innes Ireland seventh and Steve McQueen ninth.

In the twelve hour race, Steve McQueen shared the car with John Colgate. With nearly five hours gone, Steve was leading the class by a lap when the centre main bearing cap broke and the engine went rough. He brought the car into the pits and we retired it. I gave the reason for retirement as a bird through the radiator and the timers entered this on the record sheet with the comment 'hard!' DMH and I had had doubts about the wisdom of choosing a film star driver, but Ian Patterson of BMC Canada assured us that they had checked him out. In the event, Steve McQueen proved a very competent driver, well able to hold his place in the team and, contrary to his screen image, very well behaved.

We built and raced two MG Midgets, including this light alloy panelled one, shown here with two Sprites prior to Sebring 1963.

Sebring 1965: Baker in the Sprite is about to overtake a Porsche on his way to a class win.

In 1963 we ran two of the cars in the three hour race, one changed to Midget form driven by Graham Hill, and the other by Pedro Rodriguez. The special limited slip differentials broke within the first five laps. John Colgate was joined by Clive Baker on the 1098 cc coupé in the twelve hour race and they won their class ahead of the Abarths, despite the block cracking around the centre main bearing in the eleventh hour.

In 1964 the race for small GT cars was replaced by a stock car race. Baker and Colgate again beat the Abarths to win the class in the twelve hour race despite a broken oil pump, also in the eleventh hour. We filled the sump way up so that the crankshaft was submerged and they managed to run under their own power to qualify at the end.

The 1965 event saw two Sprites with 1293 cc engines. The new wind-tunnel developed model (described on page 156) was driven by Rauno Aaltonen and Clive Baker to fifteenth position overall, while the older model driven by Paddy Hopkirk finished eighteenth. We also entered a 3000 driven by Paul Hawkins and Warwick Banks, which finished in seventeenth position. A GT Midget driven by Andrew Hedges and Roger Mac finished twenty-sixth for a class win. Rain was not the most usual occurrence at sunny Sebring but at around 5 pm lightning flashed and thunder roared and the skies opened up. A

The cockpit of the Aaltonen-Baker coupé Sprite after the 1965 Sebring race, showing signs of water leaks.

Sebring 1966.

Sebring 1967: a production car modified at Warwick and driven by Roger Enever, Alec Poole and Baird, to finish eighteenth overall and third in class. This car was run as an MG Midget at other times. The hood is not standing up to the speed.

flat airfield is not well drained and great lakes formed all round the circuit. The two Sprites were then lapping faster than most of the field. The winning Chaparral scooped up a solid stream of water with its radiator intake which then flowed through the radiator and ducting to pour into the cockpit. This was a wonderful race, with Chaparral first, Ford GT40 second, Ferrari third, Shelby Cobra fourth and Porsche fifth, and our main competition in the American market, the Triumph Spitfire, way down the field.

In 1966 both Le Mans type Sprites finished first and second in the class with Timo Makinen/Paul Hawkins and Rauno Aaltonen/Clive Baker ahead of all the works Triumphs. In 1967 Baker and Aaltonen came first in the class, with Alec Poole, Carson Baird and Roger Enever third.

1968 was the last year we raced at Sebring. We modified the standard bodied Sprite to make it into an MG Midget which we entered in the sports car class with two American drivers, Jerry Truitt and Randy Canfield. BMC were looking for more publicity for the MG Midget and, of course, we had to co-operate. Clive Baker and Mike Garton were to drive the new petrol injected Sprite. After the first hour Baker brought the Sprite in, complaining of misfiring. We changed plugs, topped him up with petrol and sent him off. He did not go far before the engine cut completely. When he got the car back to the

Prior to Sebring 1968: the prototype Sprite with 1293 petrol-injected engine, an MGB GT, a Sprite transformed into an MG Midget for the sports category, and the lightweight MGC prototype. All the BMC cars finished the race. The Midget was later changed back to a Sprite and sold to John Harris of Chrysler UK as a road car.

Clive Baker testing the first of the petrol-injected Sprites at Silverstone, prior to the 1968 Sebring race where he won the class with Mike Garton, despite water in the fuel.

Sebring 1968: draining water from the petrol tank during the race. Minilite wheels were now BMC's choice for racing and rallying.

pits we found that the plugs were wet with water. Knowing that the head was liable to cracking, we took it off and at the same time discovered water in the fuel lines. The refuelling experts had done a hydraulic test on the refuelling device the night before. Obviously they had not dried it out properly, with the result that we had put a gallon of water into the car's tank when we refuelled. The rebuild and clean-out lost us two hours but the car still managed to finish first in the 1300 cc prototype class, with a lowly thirty-fifth position overall. After a trouble-free run, the Midget finished fifteenth to win the sports class and category ahead of Ed Nelson's GT 40.

In 1969 Jim Baker of Atlanta ran two of his Sprites under the Ring Free Oil Racing Team, finishing first and second in the class.

Sebring was not all hard work, the proceedings being enlivened by Fred Royston's annual party at the Kenilworth Hotel and the light-hearted horse-play of the drivers. One night a discussion developed as to whether a Mini

Dougie Watts in disguise causes a few laughs at Sebring. Automotive Products' brake and clutch expert, Roy Fenner, was not quite sure if the vision was real!

Moke would float. We had two Mokes at Sebring that year as BMC were investigating the possibility of selling this Issigonis inspired design in the USA. Timo Makinen had previously amazed the locals and the police force by demonstrating his skill on the local store's huge car park. A man of quick action, he now took the Moke and drove it into the Motel's swimming pool. It started to sink but Timo remained seated until the water covered his head. The whole team somehow manhandled the Moke out of the pool, the Motel owner taking the whole episode in good spirits despite being lumbered with a lot of work cleaning up the oil. After the race, Stuart Turner said that as it was a Sprite driver who had done the damage, Roger and I should suffer the drive back to Palm Beach in the Moke, instead of the air-conditioned Chevrolet Impala. One hundred and twenty miles in hot Florida sunshine on mediocre roads in a rough riding Moke with water in the fuel is not to be recommended.

Like the Targa Florio, Sebring no longer features on the international racing circuit. Indeed, it could not provide the same exciting spectacle without the big American Ford GT40s, the Shelby Cobras, Chaparrals and Chevrolet Stingrays. In 1978, however, after a long period of idleness, Sebring once again became a race track with a series of events including one for vintage cars. In this Stirling Moss drove Jim Rodger's Birdcage Maserati to victory: that must surely have been the height of nostalgia, to see the world's greatest driver in the legendary Birdcage, winning at Sebring again.

Le Mans

The scene of one of Europe's oldest long distance races, Le Mans is located in the *department* of Sarthe, in the middle of France. It is a pretty delapidated place, its houses looking as if they last saw a coat of paint sometime during the Great War. The race itself takes place on the Sarthe Permanent Circuit, consisting of the Avenue du Golf–a private piece of road owned by the Automobile Club de l'Ouest, and a series of well surfaced public roads.

We competed at Le Mans several times with Nash Healeys, being placed fourth in 1950, sixth in 1951, third in 1952 and eleventh in 1953. In 1953 our Austin Healey 100s came twelfth and fourteenth. In 1955 they were involved in a terrible accident, and it was to be five years before we decided to compete there again.

The 1960 race was the twenty-eighth in the series, run over a course of 13.461 kilometres ($8\frac{1}{2}$ miles). GT or production cars had to have engines in excess of 1000 cc capacity, which meant that we could not run a Sprite in standard form. Instead, we decided to run a special sports edition in the prototype category, fitted with the Falcon fibreglass body. This was light and quite quick, fitted with its 'Perspex' screen that met the FIA regulations.

We decided to run two of these Sprites and duly sent in applications before the closing date of 29th February. The first, with John Colgate and John Sprinzel as drivers, was accepted, while the second was put on the list of reserves. In May, however, only four weeks before the race, John Sprinzel had an accident in the Acropolis Rally. He doubted whether he would be fully

John Colgate driving the lightweight Sprite with Falcon body at Nassau. The wheels are all the same size, the distortion on the photograph being caused by the use of a telephoto lens. (R. Pelatowski)

recovered in time and so John Dalton took his place.

M. Acat, the Secretary General of the Automobile Club de l'Ouest, then proceeded to issue loads of bumf during which he slipped in a new regulation which stated that windscreens had to be made of laminated safety glass, such as Triplex. Dean Delamont of the Royal Automobile Club wrote to me pointing out that Le Mans could not enforce the use of glass windscreens and that this had been pointed out to the Commission Sportive Internationale, the organization that controls international motor sport. There was a great deal of correspondence on the subject, Acat being evasive and slow. Time was getting short and we knew that the French had made up their minds to exclude cars without glass screens. There is little doubt that they would have been able to produce some reason or other, the regulations containing some seventy-two articles and umpteen sub-articles. Thus we gave in and got Weathershields to build us a screen that would be accepted. The minimum depth of glass required

The simple instrument and switch layout of the 1960 Le Mans Sprite. The hydraulic brake reservoir on the left is at a high level to ensure a sufficient head of fluid to the brake system.

Digger Digby's team of signallers give the come-in sign to the Sprite as it passes the signal-
ling pits. They are also keeping a watch on another car.

ensured that this was both large and ugly, its consequent weight and drag
inflicting quite a severe penalty on a small car like the Sprite.

Cecil Winby, the British Piston Ring Company's expert, and an RAC
official scrutineer measured the engine and stamped the pistons and block,
and the RAC produced the necessary certificate. The engine, XSP1548/1,
with a bore of 64.5 mm and stroke of 76.2 mm, had a swept volume of 996 cc.
Like most of the successful BMC competition engines this was built by Eddie
Maher and his team at Morris Engines, Coventry.

As a result of the 1955 accident, the ACO had made a number of changes to
improve safety. Signalling to the cars was permitted only from signalling pits
situated after the slow corner at Mulsanne. Orders for signals were passed
from the pits by means of some very crude Great War telephone equipment
and failures were frequent.

Responsibility for signals to our team lay in the capable hands of S. J.
'Digger' Digby of Fairhead and Sawyer at Woodbridge, Austin and Austin
Healey specialists. He organised a great team of men who would travel out
from Southend, arriving at Le Mans at 7 pm on Friday and pitching camp at
the signalling pits. These volunteers did a marvellous job throughout the

twenty-four hours, for which we contributed the niggardly sum of £35 towards their expenses.

Le Mans is a protracted affair. The nucleus of the team, Roger Menadue, John Colgate, Jim Cashmore, Bill Hewitt, John Dalton, Peter Pumfrey and I flew out on Sunday from Southampton to Cherbourg with the car and equipment. We flew by Silver City, that splendid organization using Bristol Freighters, then the best and quickest method of crossing the Channel. John Colgate was shattered by the French food which he did not enjoy and we hoped that he would be hardened off by race time. The next day we arrived at the Hotel du Croissant at Cerans Foulletourte, our base for the week. We were welcomed by the proprietor, M. L'Hermitte, who had organized everything as requested in my letters. The girls were obviously pleased to see Roger.

Scrutineering for us was at 7.15 am on Tuesday, which should have allowed us plenty of time for any changes before first practice on Wednesday evening. Of course, we arrived on time, only to find that the officials were not fully awake. We had to produce all the forms, the certificate of roadworthiness from the RAC, the certificate of engine capacity, entrants' and drivers' licences and the special insurance certificate for the drivers. The scrutineers at the various stations filled in forms, measured with string and sticks and were obviously delighted with the monstrous windscreen. Major Harold Parker of the RAC hovered around in case of difficulty but the car was passed with little comment. The French officials would not speak English and I would not speak French. Our greatest difficulty was to persuade them not to place their stamp on some critical piece of equipment. They have been known to wreck a dynamo when thumping their steel stamp, blunted by years of use, with a 4 lb hammer near to the end bracket. We also had the spare dynamo and starter stamped.

When all the verification operations were finally completed, there would start the haggle over passes. Acat would give me an envelope with a small number of passes and I would complain to the interpreter and show him our crew list. He would grumble and produce three more. This went on until we had enough. I was always amazed that it was so difficult to get sufficient crew passes, when on race day the pit area would swarm with people often totally unconnected with the cars. We just managed to complete operations before the long French lunch break occurred.

After that there was nothing to do until the next evening, apart from arranging for the Hotel to feed us on our return after Wednesday's practice at about midnight. Those who had not been into Le Mans went in for a look around. Most do this once only.

We practised on Wednesday without any drama, the car and driver satisfying the officials on performance. At nightfall, the Lucas men adjusted the lights and the drivers had a few small alterations made. After enough laps in daylight and in the dark, the drivers said they were satisfied and that they would not want to practise on Thursday night. We had checked and calculated the fuel consumption and made a record of all the lap times. Roger and the crew then loaded the spares and the car and we returned to base. After a quick wash and a few drinks, we sat down to a colossal meal at midnight.

Early the next morning we had eggs and bacon and coffee for breakfast and then started preparing the car for Saturday's race. We measured all the brake pads and calculated the probable life. Dunlop's light car disc brakes were very good and would easily cover the twenty-four hours without a pad change, while their 525-13 racing tyres looked good enough to last two Le Mans races. The mechanics changed the oils and oil filter, torqued down the cylinder head and adjusted the tappets. At the drivers' request, some extra Dunlop foam rubber was also glued onto certain parts of the gearbox tunnel.

Ray Wood of Lucas arrived to check the electrics. Lucas had already organized this back at Warwick but they always carried out an additional pre-race check, to make sure that the wiring had not been altered subsequently, in a potentially hazardous fashion. On one occasion the drivers had the rev counter turned so that it was easier to read at night. This caused the ignition warning light to short circuit on some piece of metal, resulting in a burnt out dynamo in practice. If this had happened during the race, it would have been put down to electrical failure of a Lucas dynamo.

With Roger, I then sat down and listed out the food for the race, which M. L'Hermitte would have ready early on Saturday. This consisted mainly of hard boiled eggs, ham, salad, bread, water and soft drinks, together with our own supply of tea and condensed milk. The signallers arrived at 7 pm that Friday evening and with the drivers we agreed on the signalling codes to be employed. We all then enjoyed a leisurely meal and a quantity of M. L'Hermitte's special Calvados. This helped one sleep – and sleep in that roadside hotel was difficult the night before the race. Some moronic competitor spent most of the night testing his noisy misfiring car up and down the road to Le Mans. It was obviously a very sick device and lasted only a few laps the next day.

The next morning, we all had a good breakfast of bacon and eggs, cooked to our instructions in the English way, and set out for the track. On race day, it takes an hour to cover the 15 miles to the track if you leave at 9.30. If you start later and the French police do their traffic disorganization exercise, it can take considerably longer.

The cars have to be in front of the pits at midday when various officials check points and fill in yet more forms. Between 2.30 and 3 pm the tanks are filled and sealed by the *plombeurs*. Derek Ross was in charge of our refuelling, a job he carried out with great precision, getting the tanks full without spilling a drop. It was important not to waste any fuel as this would have been recorded against the car and would impair its chances in the index of thermal efficiency. The

Dunlop technicians made a final check of tyre pressures and the car was wheeled to its starting position. This position is determined by the fastest lap times in practice, the fastest car being placed at the top end of the pits and the remainder in order of descending speed down to the slowest at the bottom end. This type of start has since fallen into disfavour, being considered a safety hazard.

Next the engines were warmed up and John Colgate, our first driver, told us how he wanted the car to be left. As is normally the case, this was in first gear with the handbrake off. At 3.50 all engines have to be stopped and the drivers take up their positions, standing in circles opposite their cars on the other side of the track. At 4 pm the starter drops his flag and the race is on. The drivers sprint across the track, open the doors of the cars and with luck start up immediately. The cars have to be started by means of the normal electrical starter. No other method, such as using a handle or pushing, is permitted.

The initial stages of Le Mans are always the most exciting, when the cars are running at high speed and the lead is constantly changing. By the end of the first hour the Sprite was forty-ninth out of the fifty-five starters and second in the class. It continued to run with monotonous regularity, stopping to refuel and change drivers every 2 hours 50 minutes. Here the importance of having a frugal Scot like Derek Ross in charge really showed. He would fill the car quickly and meticulously, only signing the official form after he had carefully checked the meter readings. The Sprite had a good chance of winning the thermal efficiency prize.

In the third hour it started to rain and the Sprite gradually gained on the class leader, taking the lead in the fifth hour. Night came and things quietened down, the number of curious visitors decreasing with each pit stop. Dunlop, Lucas, Mintex and Smith experts hovered round in case any advice was needed. At dawn, Ray Wood came in to say that Lucas would be brewing tea and frying eggs at seven and that any of the crew were welcome to partake. All the time cars were dropping out with burnt valves, electrical failures, broken clutches, gearboxes and run bearings. Continental cars seem to suffer badly with electrical failures.

The day gradually warmed up and we took it in turns to stand at the back of the pits in the sun. With two hours to go the Sprite came in for a final pit stop. We had a slight problem. A very severe oil leak had developed at the filter joint and the engine had started to pump oil into the clutch housing. This was a familiar problem with the early Sprites, which all showed a tendency to pass oil through the rear seal when the main bearings were subjected to a certain amount of wear. Roger employed the old palliative of squirting the contents of a Pyrene extinguisher through a hole onto the clutch. A new joint liberally coated with Hylomar was fitted between the filter and the cylinder block, and John Dalton was instructed to keep the revs down on the last stint, to reduce the oil pumping.

I phoned our signallers at Mulsanne and told them what had happened. Digger and his alert crew kept in touch with the drivers and the pits, keeping a set of lap times in addition to their signalling duties. We still had a good lead in the class but from now on they had to watch for the OK signal from John. As the end drew near, we had a constant battle to keep the pits free of the hordes of gawpers and souvenir hunters, at the same time trying to let in our numerous friends. It was vital to be alert until the end in case of an unscheduled pit stop. Fortunately there was no further incident and John crossed the line neck and neck with the only other BMC car in the race, an MGA twin cam entered by Ted Lund with Colin Escott as co-driver. This had been bored out to 1762 cc and was run with modified bodywork, extending the top rearwards to improve wind resistance. John brought the car back to the pits for the last time where the tank was topped up, sealed and wheeled away for a final weight check by the scrutineers.

The official results for the Sprite were good, though at Le Mans everyone seems to win something, whether it be a class or a formula. The Sprite was twentieth overall, having covered a distance of 3307.438 km (2055.142 miles). It came eleventh on the index of performance, fifth on the index of thermal efficiency, first in the 1000 cc sports car class, and twelfth overall in the sports car class. Its best lap was at 91.15 mph, compared with 99.46 mph achieved by the MGA. Some measure of the improvement in performance of sports cars generally can be gauged from the fact that the Sprite had covered a greater distance than the winning Ferrari of the 1949 race.

After the race we packed up and waited for the crowds to disperse before going back to the hotel for a quiet celebration. Everyone was tired after some thirty-six hours at the circuit and members of the team kept dropping off over the meal. On Monday morning we left for Cherbourg and the Silver City flight back to Southampton. The whole trip had taken eight days, with the mechanics having an extra day off to make up for a lost weekend.

Back at Warwick I sat down to check the results and found an error in the calculations for the index of thermal efficiency. I wrote to Acat pointing this out to him and he replied that the statisticians had not strictly applied the regulations. In arriving at this classification, they had taken into account not the distance covered during the twenty-four hours but the complete number of circuits. He promised to let me know the result of the revised classification but that was the last I heard of the matter. We should have been fourth not fifth on the overall classification of the index of thermal efficiency, not a very important improvement. We had undoubtedly achieved the main aim of the exercise, however, successfully demonstrating that the Sprite was a true sports car. And being Le Mans, it obtained wide publicity.

The first coupé, ready for the Le Mans 24 Hour Race in the yard of the Hotel du Croissant. Essentially a coupé version of the open special, it had a blind spot which was reduced by the addition of windows in the rear quarter panels.

For the 1961 Le Mans, we built a new car with fully enclosed bodywork. This was the first of a series of closed Sprites which we were to build for racing, and particularly for Le Mans, up till 1968. In addition, David Murray of Ecurie Ecosse talked us into building a car for Ninian Sanderson and his new driver McKay. Ninian had won the 1965 Le Mans on a D Type Jaguar with Ron Flockhart. Our car was to be driven by John Colgate and Paul Hawkins, who in addition to being an excellent driver was a first rate racing mechanic.

The 1961 Le Mans Sprite, built to specification number ST461, utilized the basic understructure of the car we had raced in 1960. In place of the Falcon body, Les Ireland designed a new body, based on the design of the open XQHS car, with an all aluminium top. This was built at our factory at the Cape in Warwick. The Ecurie Ecosse Sprite was the one with which Walt Hansgen had finished second in the four-hour race at Sebring earlier that year, fitted with a new hard top and a lengthened nose. Eddie Maher rebuilt two of the Sebring units, XSP1736-2 and XSP1736-4, each with a certified capacity of 994 cc.

The 1961 Le Mans race was a failure for us. Colgate lapped steadily at 92 mph and Paul Hawkins, who took over just after 7 pm, kept up the same pace. By 9 pm the car was twenty-ninth on the index and forty-first overall, having completed fifty-two laps. At 9.40 pm Paul came into the pits with one cylinder out of action. We fitted a new set of plugs and sent him away. Laurie Hands of Champion examined the plugs and discovered that number three was fouled, indicating a fault in the engine. Sure enough, Paul stopped at the pits on the next lap. We whipped out the plugs and Laurie used his special light to look into number three cylinder. After much juggling the crankshaft was turned to the appropriate position, enabling us to look through the plug hole. This immediately revealed a hole in the piston. We debated the possibility of fitting a new piston but a simple calculation showed that if we did this in the quickest possible time we could not have covered the regulation minimum number of laps by 4 am. This would have meant automatic elimination and so, sadly, the car was driven away to the back of the pits. On his first stint on the Ecurie Ecosse Sprite, McKay lost it at White House and that was the end of that. The race was won by Olivier Gendebien and Phil Hill with an average speed of 115.9 mph.

Pistons are holed for a variety of reasons but it was a most uncommon occurrence on the Sprite engine. The engines had been tested and adjusted to

The old experimental shop at the Cape Works, with two coupé Sprites and one production model.

suit the Le Mans fuel in Coventry and the plugs had shown no signs of any malfunction in practice. The thickness of the piston crown was increased in future engines and I never saw another failure like this. Mike Garton later bought this Sprite and enjoyed a lot of success racing it.

We missed the 1962 race and for 1963 built another coupé. The front end was simplified and the tail finished in the well known sawn-off fashion, devised by Kamm. The theory is that if you cannot make the tail very long with a gentle slope to avoid the air flow breaking away, you might as well cut it off. It also provided a nice flat panel for the rear race number. BMC's Competitions Department offered us two of their top racing drivers: John Whitmore and Bob Olthoff, an offer we were pleased to accept.

The small changes made to the bodywork and the increased output of the engine were sufficient for the drivers to lap in excess of 100 mph for the first time in practice. It looked as though the car would do well. In the race it ran well at an average speed of just under 100 mph until just after 1 am on the Sunday, when Bob Olthoff had an accident at White House. There was no question that Bob was going too fast and he claimed that he was momentarily dazzled as he entered the corner. The French officials claimed that this was not possible as photographers were not permitted to use flash lights. However some very clear pictures of the wreck later appeared in the French papers, obviously taken on some French film that can be used in complete darkness.

When the car did not appear on time we got worried and phoned Digger at the signal pits. He told us the car had passed through minutes before and that the driver had acknowledged his signal. We asked the officials if they knew anything, with negative results. Then Vito, the Weber carburettor representative, came in and told us the car had crashed at White House. I went to race headquarters to try to find out if the driver was OK but all the officials seemed totally unconcerned and again denied any knowledge of an accident involving our car. Maurice Wilks, the boss of Rover who were running their remarkable gas turbine engined car, overheard my enquiries and kindly offered to help. He then came back with a piece of paper saying that Bob Olthoff was in a certain hospital in Le Mans.

So, with John Whitmore and Bob's wife, we went to the hospital. Bob was badly bruised and dazed but we could not get any real medical information. We decided that the sooner we got him back to England for proper attention the better. Fortunately a British businessman, G. R. Dawes, said that he could fly Bob back if we got him to the airfield at 4 pm. This was arranged and Bob made a rapid recovery in Britain. The hospital at Le Mans sent us a bill for two days' hospitalization at some exorbitant rate: I told the insurance company to pay for only the one day.

For 1964 we entered another Sprite coupé. We built the body on the wooden buck formerly used for the 1964 Targa Florio car, but used a one-piece front-

The steel understructure, spray-painted in aluminium, for one of the early coupés, in the experimental department at the Cape. The corrugated iron curtain kept out customers and the service department.

hinged bonnet for easier access to the power unit. Our drivers this year were Clive Baker and Bill Bradley. Clive was a talented driver who gave the impression that he never took anything seriously, an attitude that prevented his progress in the racing world. Bill was both experienced and serious and was able to instill some sense into him. Following our disastrous outing in 1961

155

The 1964 Le Mans coupé. The bug deflector did help, although the later very powerful Lucas screen wipers and washers, aided by Trico's solvent, made it unnecessary. The low air intake and oil cooler were very effective.

and 1963, we decided to go for a finishing place. The two drivers drove well within their capabilities, finishing twenty-fourth.

The maximum speed of the Sprites was limited by poor aerodynamics. After the 1964 Le Mans we decided to seek the help of Doc Weaving at Austin who agreed that two of the cars should be tested in wind tunnels. The 1964 Targa Florio and Le Mans cars were driven over to the Austin Research Department in the East Works at Longbridge, where Graham Page and John Ebrey somehow found time to do some tests on them as delivered. They used smoke candles to determine the airflow over the body and the point where breakaway occurred. Next they built up the body with plastic foam and cut this to shape to improve the airflow. This showed that the Targa Florio car could be improved, with an increase in maximum speed from 125 to 136 mph. The 1964 Le Mans car indicated a maximum speed of 132 mph which was in

A later coupé understructure showing the semi-elliptic rear springs. These coupé bodies were very rigid.

line with the performance obtained.

Time was short and they told us what we needed to improve performance:

1. Remove the sharp corner around the windscreen.
2. Fair the side windows into the general shape.
3. Keep the maximum height of the roof line as near the front as possible.
4. Have a gentle slope to the rear.
5. Reduce the radiator intake area and use a full undertray.
6. Reduce the frontal area as much as possible.

The FIA regulations imposed a minimum windscreen size and I drew this on the existing windscreen. We had used the Austin Mini windscreen in preference to that on the production Sprites as it had a better, less flattened curve. I then talked to Triplex who made all our screen glasses: their windscreens were optically superior to those produced by their competitors. They

Austin wind tunnel tested the 1964 Targa Florio and Le Mans Sprites in January 1965. The car modified by the addition of rigid foam was the base from which we developed the 1965–8 Le Mans Sprites. The short metal top was added to the car after the 1964 Targa Florio.

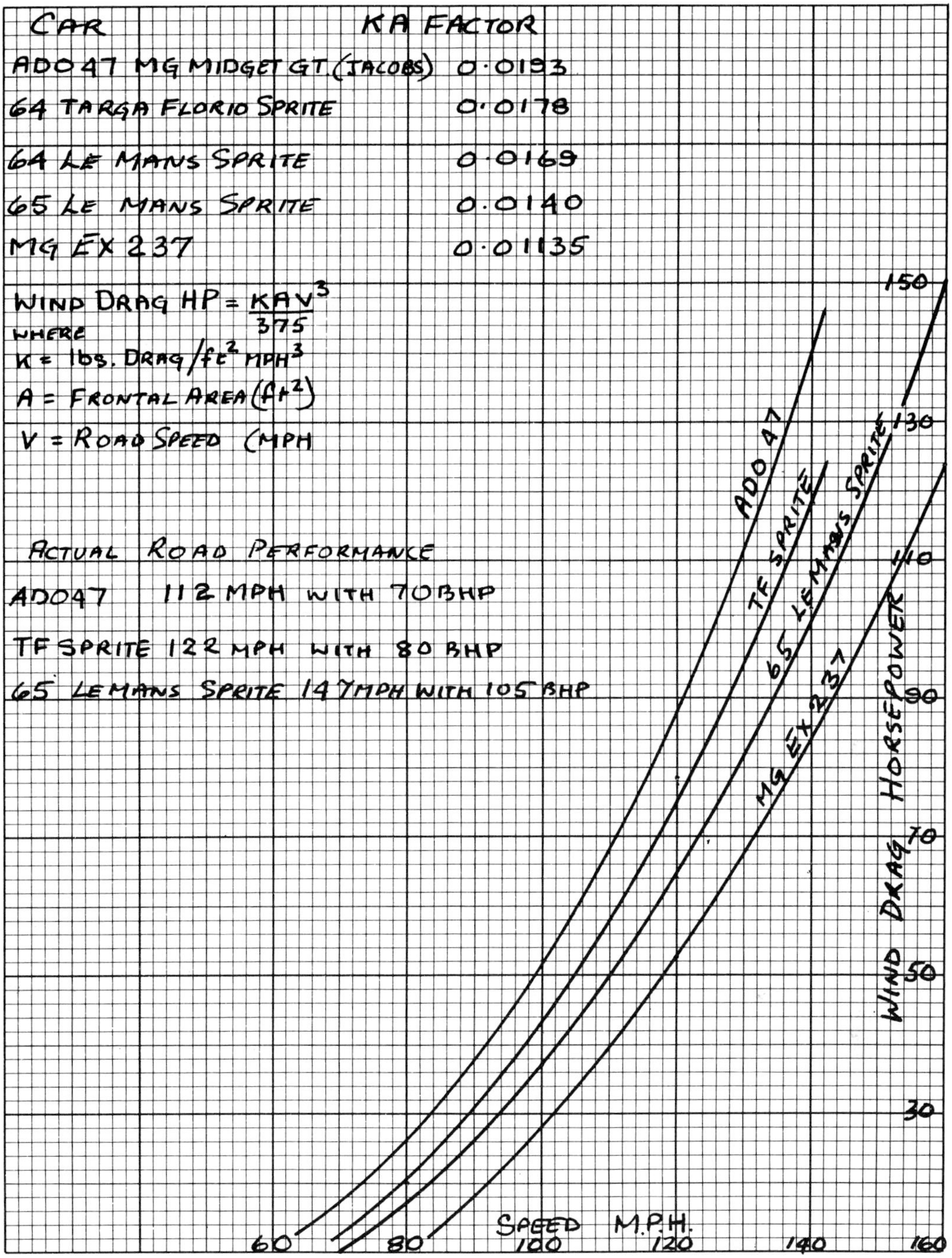
CAR
KA FACTOR
ADO 47 MG MIDGET GT (JACOBS) 0·0193
64 TARGA FLORIO SPRITE 0·0178
64 LE MANS SPRITE 0·0169
65 LE MANS SPRITE 0·0140
MG EX 237 0·01135
WIND DRAG HP = KAV³/375
WHERE
K = lbs. DRAG/ft² MPH³
A = FRONTAL AREA (ft²)
V = ROAD SPEED (MPH
ACTUAL ROAD PERFORMANCE
ADO47 112 MPH WITH 70BHP
TF SPRITE 122 MPH WITH 80 BHP
65 LEMANS SPRITE 147MPH WITH 105 BHP
ADO 47
TF SPRITE
65 LE MANS SPRITE
MG EX 237
WIND DRAG HORSEPOWER
150
130
110
90
70
50
30
SPEED M.P.H.
60
80
100
120
140
160

Wind tunnel results on the Spridget. Small development alterations to the cars enabled them to exceed the predicted performance.

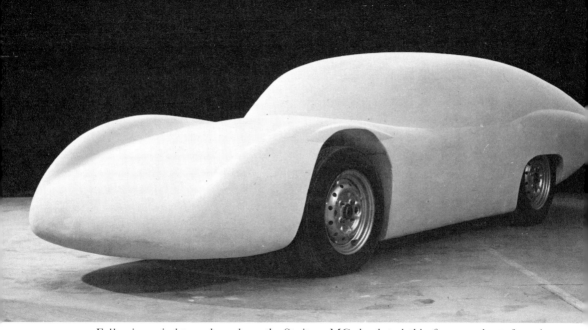

Following wind tunnel work on the Sprites, MG developed this foam mock-up for a low drag MG–EX237.

Bill Buckingham panelled nearly all the racing Sprites. Here he rasps the surface of the body to smooth it and provide a key for the paint. He would normally use both hands on the rasp.

The 1968 Le Mans Sprite on display at Earls Court International Motor Show, with the Jaguar-Coventry Climax Trophy won by mechanics Jim Cashmore in 1967 and Roger Menadue in 1968. Austin built the very fine turntable for this eye-catching display. (Austin Morris)

1974 Midget with the commonized Sprite grille. Note that the rear wheel arch has reverted to a design similar to that on the original Sprite. Later the deeper MG-inspired wheel arch of the MkII and MkIII models was re-introduced to provide additional strength to meet new US legislation following rear end impact tests. (Austin Morris)

The first of the wind tunnel developed Sprites, photographed at Warwick shortly after completion. This car was used in the 1965 Sebring race. The wheels were cribbed from Kjell Qvale's BMCD alloy type.

agreed to cut down some old Mini tools to produce the form we required, thus saving us both time and money. Dunlop provided a suitable adhesive so that the screen could be bonded into the frame, thereby avoiding any obstructions to the airflow and at the same time adding to the body strength.

I roughed out the lines that the car should have and Barry Bilbie and Derek Westwood laid them out. Doug Green and Bernard Foster, Barford builders, made up the wooden subframe and cut the frame sections out for us. Terry Westwood, Derek's brother, assembled the sections in the small body shop and faired in the lines. Then Terry and Bill Buckingham proceeded to form the metal panels from Birmabright, an aluminium alloy that work-hardened to give a strength close to body sheet steel with, of course, a considerable saving in weight. Panel beating–the hammering and rolling of the flat sheet into complex curves–is one of the most skilled arts in the metal industry and it is also hard work. After some fifty years on the game, Bill was very deaf.

In the experimental shop, Jim Cashmore, Mike Guest and Clive Hendry were building up the understructure based on the production Sprite under-frame, as produced by John Thompson Motor Pressings. The steel floors and some of the footwell panels were cut out and replaced with a hard grade of

Birmabright which was glued with araldite and rivetted in to retain the strength.

Phipps Plastics moulded the Perspex light covers on moulds we supplied. For the rear screen we used a new material, Cobex, which we could fit to the curved shape without moulding. It was flexible and did not crack easily. The body panels were next fitted to the underframe, again using Araldite, pop-rivetting and a flexible adhesive made by Addshead Ratcliffe. We used a great variety of adhesives over the years during our search for the perfect one.

When we had completed the car we took it to Longbridge for a check. The results of a quick wind tunnel test indicated that it was better than had been anticipated and we decided to enter two for the next Le Mans, 1965. Our two pairs of drivers were Rauno Aaltonen and Clive Baker, and Paul Hawkins and John Rhodes.

The appearance of the new cars at Le Mans produced an immediate reaction from the officials. Here was something that could pose a threat to the highly developed small French sports cars and the Sprites were subjected to a very thorough scrutineering. Finding nothing that contravened the rules, the scrutineers suddenly said that the colour of the cars gave us an unfair advantage and that they should be painted in the national colour, British Racing Green.

Le Mans scrutineers using string and a piece of wood to measure something, while Jim Cashmore looks worried.

Le Mans

ASSOCIATION SPORTIVE
DE
L'AUTOMOBILE-CLUB DE L'OUEST

13, BOULEVARD RENÉ-LEVASSEUR – LE MANS

TÉLÉPHONE
28.54.57

C. C. P. NANTES 88-48

B. P. 126 LE MANS

NOTE pour Monsieur Donald HEALEY concernant les voitures AUSTIN HEALEY N° 48 _ 49

=•••••••••••••••=

Nous avons l'honneur de vous faire connaître que le Collège des Commissaires Sportifs des 24 HEURES DU MANS 1965, ~~ayant~~ constaté que la peinture dont vous vous êtes servi pour vos voitures est fluorescente.

Cette pratique qui peut présenter des dangers quant à la sécurité générale de l'épreuve ne peut être autorisée, nous vous prions de bien vouloir modifier la nature de la peinture employée afin de supprimer tout caractère fluorescent.

Les Commissaires Sportifs :

The letter signed by the six Commissaires Sportifs at Le Mans, in which they claimed that the Sprites' paintwork was dangerous.

163

I retaliated by pointing out the appropriate paragraph in the regulations, which stated that cars *should* be painted in national colours but did not use the mandatory word *must*. Time went by and in the end I was called into a special enclosure. Harold Parker of the RAC, who was there to assist British competitors, was not permitted to accompany me. Here I was presented with a letter signed by the six top officials, stating that the College of Commissaires had ruled that the paint was fluorescent and this presented dangers. I argued that for a small car to be clearly visible was a safety factor, pointing out that the drivers of small cars were always aware of the danger of being run over by the bigger, much faster cars in conditions of poor visibility. They were adamant, continually repeating the word 'danger' like parrots. I do not think that they would have gone to the extent of excluding us but we would have been placed in a very difficult position if, after they had stated that the paintwork was dangerous, we had been involved in an accident.

There were now two courses open to me–either to repaint the cars or to say to hell with it and withdraw. I discussed the matter with the team who promised me their wholehearted support whichever course I decided to take. However, it was clear that they had put a great deal of effort into the operation and would be disappointed if we did not run. There was also a large British contingent who had come to see the Sprites perform. So we agreed to repaint the cars.

Now all the screaming and squawking about this dangerous paint had become public and I had great difficulty in persuading any paint shop to repaint the cars. In the end I found a small shop who agreed to do the work, providing I obtained a non cellulose paint. In a store I found a gallon of green paint which had probably been swiped from the US Army during the war. The proprietor insisted we only delivered one car at a time for painting, with the petrol tank drained, and treated the thing like an unexploded bomb. The job took an awfully long time: before he started the painter squirted fire extinguisher fluid all over the car, the engine and in the oil and petrol tanks, and the paint was very slow drying. We had a pretty stiff bill for carrying out an operation '*Tres dangereux*' and the mechanics had a lot of additional work clearing the systems of fire extinguisher fluid.

When he saw the car and the bill, Paul Hawkins said something to the effect that he could get a better job done by a drunken kangaroo in half the time at a tenth of the cost. Even in today's liberal climate it is unfortunately impossible to put Paul's exact words on paper. Colin Chapman had a similar run in with the organizers over a Lotus which would have won the index of performance, a French prerogative: he never returned to Le Mans.

As an exhausted but determined crew lined up the cars for the start, we knew we had been *psyched*. The cars went like trains, recording 147 mph on the straight on the official timing. On the Sunday morning the Aaltonen/Baker car broke with a bang as it passed the pits. Subsequent examination of the

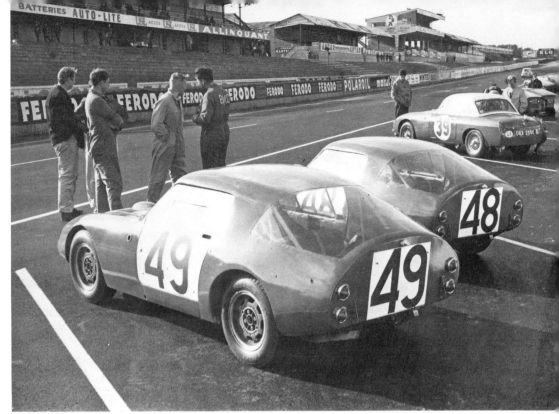

Le Mans 1965: two Sprites and one MGB ready for first practice. In the group are Derek Ross, Clive Hendrie, Jim Cashmore and Tommy Wellman.

wrecked engine suggested that the distributor drive gear had worn and broken, being expelled through the side of the crankcase. It is difficult to be sure but this unusual failure could have been caused by contamination during the re-painting process. The other car, driven superbly by Paul Hawkins and John Rhodes, finished a creditable twelfth overall, at the same time beating the French opposition to win its class. Cleaned up by Austin's paint experts, this car was later displayed at the Motor Show. I am sure that if we had not been so badly treated both cars would have finished much higher up the field.

Timekeeping is an essential part of racing. It is important to know how fast one's cars are lapping, the performance of their rivals in the class and the overall position. For years this was done with a mixture of stop watches, Huer, Smiths and other reliable makes. Pit space is always limited and the timers' view was often obscured by bodies, official and otherwise! Various methods were adopted to keep the time sheets and watches dry. In some of the continental downpours, the watches would become waterlogged and my old friend Trevor Vage of Truro would spend many hours rebuilding and recalibrating them. One favourite watch always seemed to be the least waterproof.

Spotters looked out for the cars and noted their passing. The timer, seated on some makeshift structure, would record the passing and note the lap time on the time sheets. We were always very fortunate to have the services of some top class timers such as Peter Browning, Les Needham, Andrew Wilson Gunn, my brother Bic and many others. It is a demanding task: I remember one so-called expert putting his pen down with a weary sigh after the first half hour and stating 'I've lost it!'–and what a mess he had made. The various formulae involved in some of Le Mans' complicated indices required laborious calculations, though often one could only guess at the position.

Sebring had always run a very efficient team under Joe Lane and were quick in passing out their hourly sheets. The organizers then decided to improve the service and installed an IBM computer. Fed with details by Joe's team, this was able to produce volumes of accurate information on all cars, including lap speed, race average, position overall, in the class and in the various indices. Following the success of the Sebring computer operation, Le Mans decided to go one better and for 1966 fully automated the operation. IBM again installed a computer and in addition each car was fitted with a battery powered sender which signalled the car's passing over a cable to the timing stand, where the signal was identified and timed and a card perforated and fed into the computer. The results went first to the press stand and were ultimately delivered by boy scouts to the individual race pits. Of course each team continued to employ a back-up team of its own timers, for however well the official timing and distribution worked it would always be too slow for the men in the pits.

Unfortunately, we did not get much benefit from the computerized system in its first year, as both the Sprites we had entered broke down before the end of the race. The two cars were identical to the 1965 models, with the addition of GKN Laycock overdrive units on the gear boxes, based on the MGB design. This was the only time that we fitted overdrive to the Sprite. The arrangement gave us six speeds and helped to push up the lap speeds. We also made small detail improvements to the oil system and obtained a higher standard of finish to the bodies.

Both cars failed with broken connection rods after covering very similar distances–at approximately $19\frac{1}{2}$ hours. The rods broke at the same point, at a stress raising corner under the bolt head. This type of coincidence is common when identical cars are run. As a result, the production rods were improved –another instance by which owners benefited from factory involvement in racing. The failures may also have been due in part to oil passing through the crankshaft seals and getting on the clutches, causing intermittent slip.

Failure in a race always depresses a team's spirit, particularly when it occurs so close to the end of a race. Up to the point of failure the performance of the cars had been excellent, with a race average of 101.3 mph and a fastest lap of 107.99 mph, with a good position on the index. On the long straight the cars touched 150 mph. Some brake trouble was experienced with the experimental Lockheed rear disc brakes when one of the drivers used the hand brake

Andrew Hedges cornering the Sprite at Le Mans. The adjustable air intake is about three-quarters open. At night the scoop would be closed to keep the engine temperature up, and the protective tape and paper lamp covers removed.

to try to induce the rear end to move out. When subjected to this unusual technique, the partly worn pads promptly escaped from their retainers.

Somewhat wearily the team returned to M. L'Hermitte's Hotel du Croissant for a meal and some drinks. An obnoxious female who was present kept making snide remarks about the drivers and the cars. She went too far at the wrong moment, when M. L'Hermitte produced a series of strawberry and cream pies on large plates. By then thoroughly exasperated, Andrew Hedges took one and rammed it in her face! She departed properly silenced and this cheered the team up considerably.

On the return trip on the Thorensen Viking ferry, we ran into a group of English supporters travelling under the unlikely banner of the Leeds and Keighley Temperance Society. Under the leadership of Bryn Watson they proceeded to cheer the team up with their unconsumed rations of booze. This group was one of a number of English supporters who went each year to Le Mans, usually taking their own supplies of beer, in the hope of cheering home a British car.

1967 saw us at Le Mans once more, with one Sprite driven by Andrew Hedges and Clive Baker. Tony Cross, Girling's competition manager, had come up with a racing brake set for us, using the light alloy AR front and NR rear calipers. Twin mastercylinders with an adjustable balance bar enabled us to vary the front to rear braking ratio to suit conditions. The AR front calipers let us use larger front discs and with Mintex XM48 linings we had a powerful system with a long life between pad changes. Eddie Maher and his men at Morris Engines had developed the 1292 cc Sprite engine to a high state of reliability and had produced a special gear box based on the MGB B series unit. A special housing was necessary to fit the rear extension, incorporating a fifth overdrive ratio, giving us five speeds with strength and only a small weight penalty.

The 1967 race was dominated by Ford with their 7 litre MkIV cars. The official timers clocked the Ford of Andretti at over 213 mph and the Sprite at 146. Some of the smallest cars barely exceeded 110 mph, resulting in a colossal speed differential between them and the Fords. Their drivers had to be especially careful not to obstruct the very fast cars. Ford's line-up of drivers was impressive: Gurney/Foyt, McLaren/Donohue, Bianchi/Andretti, Hulme/Ruby, Gardner/McClusky, Schlesser/Ligier, Hawkins/Bucknum and Salmon/Redman.

Somehow, and there are a variety of stories, Clive Baker damaged the rear of

Le Mans 1967: on its way to winning the Motor Trophy, the Andrew Hedges/Clive Baker Sprite passes the wreckage of a Ford GT40 as a Ferrari driver lines up to squirt it past. (Brian Foley)

the Sprite in the esses. Dion Pears did a painting of the incident with the No. 1 Ford of Gurney and Foyt breathing down his neck. At the time there were wrecks and bits of cars all over the place and Clive did well to get through. The damage took some time to repair and dropped our race average. At the end of the twenty-four hours the Sprite had covered 2421.5 miles, giving an average of 100.91 mph. This made it the first of our cars to exceed 100 mph for the distance. It consumed 120 gallons of fuel to give an average of over 20 mpg, while the Fords were consuming fuel at the rate of 6 to 7 mpg. The Sprite finished in fifteenth position overall and was awarded the Motor Trophy as the first British car. We had first won this trophy with the Nash Healey in 1952.

The race was won by Dan Gurney and A. J. Foyt at a phenomenal average of 135.48 mph. Mike Parkes and Ludovico Scarfiotti came second with a

A celebration after Le Mans. Wearing Tommy Wellman's hat reversed, I had been telling tales of the 'old days and drivers' while Old Bull Ross, the refueller, keeps at it!

4 litre Ferrari prototype. The performance of the Fords worried the French organizers, as the spectre of the 1955 disaster still lingered.

For 1968, a chicane and pit entry lane were introduced to reduce the speed past the pits. This was a definite improvement to the safety of those working in the pits. It also reduced the lap speeds considerably, as the drivers had to go down through the gears on their approach to the chicane and accelerate up through them afterwards.

Our entry for 1968 was subject to a new arrangement with the BMC Competitions Department. Under this, BMC supplied the drivers under their contract and paid their expenses, leaving us with more money to spend on the cars. Our drivers were to be Roger Enever and Alex Poole, two of the best Sprite drivers of all time and also two of the best behaved drivers one could hope to have. The 1968 Le Mans Sprite was fitted with a new unit with Lucas petrol injection. It is unfortunate that this system could only be used on the very last race cars and was never included on the production models.

During Eddie Maher's development work on the engine, he had reached 120 bhp at around 7500 rpm, but there were problems with heads cracking. Tuftride treatment of the heads reduced this tendency but for long distance races the power was reduced by lowering the compression ratio to 11.9 to 1 and limiting the maximum engine speed to 7000 rpm. Syd Enever ran one of the engines on the MG test bed prior to the race, to determine whether we had the best camshaft and whether it was possible to lean off the strength of the fuel/air mixture. We ended up with a camshaft having a 320° opening period for both inlet and exhaust as it was felt that this gave the valves an easier life than the shorter exhaust period camshaft. In Le Mans tune the engine gave 110 bhp at 7000 rpm, some 5 bhp more than the 1967 Weber carburettor engine. More significantly, the Lucas fuel injection system gave much more power in the middle range of 4000 to 6500 rpm and its throttle response was instantaneous under all conditions. It did not blubber or hiccup under cornering forces and its precise metering gave better economy.

The petrol injection equipment meant that we had to move the dynamo to the only possible position above the cylinder head on the left-hand side. This entailed a disfiguring bulge on the bonnet to provide clearance. We used two different formations to try to reduce wind resistance. Originally we had two bulges, one for the dynamo and one for the intake trumpet clearance. These were later merged. The intake air scoop below the nose of the car was increased.

Dunlop produced their new 5.25 M tyres in wet and dry compound in place of the 500 L we had used in 1967. These gave improved cornering power and increased life. The slightly increased rolling radius of the M section gave a theoretical maximum of 148 mph at 7000 rpm against the 145 mph of the L section used in 1967. Dunlop always seemed to have the edge on the opposition with their sports car racing tyres, especially where safety and wet grip were

Alec Poole drifting the 1968 Lucas petrol-injected Sprite at Silverstone. The two bumps on the bonnet were reduced and blended into a single hump before the Le Mans race. Another good shot by a BMC photographer.

concerned. With the backing of their racing service under Dick Jeffrey and his technical representatives Alec Meskell, Ian Mills and Mike Clatworthy, we had no need to worry about tyres.

In 1968 France was in a fairly chaotic state, and for some time it seemed doubtful whether the race would take place. After much deliberation the organizers finally obtained government approval to run it at the end of September.

Dan Daley of MAT Transport obtained our bookings on the Thorensen Viking from Southampton to Le Havre for Monday night, 23rd September, and I persuaded the organizers to agree to scrutineer the cars at 2 pm on the Tuesday. The French are at their most amiable after lunch.

We left Warwick in convoy at 5.30 pm, picking up the MG contingent at Abingdon and proceeding to Southampton to assemble at the Berni Inn for a square meal. After a comfortable voyage we passed through customs at Le Havre and arrived at scrutineering where we were given the easiest and most agreeable treatment we had ever received in nearly twenty years of Le Mans events.

In addition to the Sprite we were running the SR with the Climax engine for the first time. Wally Hassan and Harry Spear of Climax came along to provide the technical expertise to enable us to get the best out of this magnificent engine. Les Needham, general secretary of the Austin Healey Club, and Peter Browning were in charge of the timekeeping while Alan Zafer covered the entire public relations and press function on behalf of BMC. An absolute master of the art, Alan obtained superb results with the minimum of inconvenience to the team.

Practice on the Wednesday evening was uneventful. The new chicane before the pits drastically slowed lap times, the additional braking and use of first gear, followed by acceleration through the gears, adding 15 seconds to the times of the smaller cars. Alec Poole and Roger Enever covered a total of twenty-three laps in practice – enough for them to qualify comfortably and to

John Harris on the SR and Alec Poole in the Sprite on Silverstone track, prior to the 1968 Le Mans Race. The SR used the Coventry Climax 2 litre V8 that put British racing cars in front.

A night stop at Le Mans for a pad change for the 1968 Le Mans Sprite that won the Motor Trophy, driven by Alec Poole and Roger Enever. (Hanchard)

start the race with some confidence. I was able to assess the fuel consumption, brake pad and tyre wear and plan the pit stop intervals for refuelling and pad changes.

Because of the lateness of the season, the organizers had advanced the start from the traditional 4 pm to 3 pm. We were also in the wet season, which meant that the cars started on a wet track. Roger Enever took up his position, along with the drivers of the fifty-three other cars. Fifty-four cars, each with two drivers, together with twelve reserve drivers, adds up to 120 drivers: and it is always a matter of concern to the top men that it is simply not possible to assemble that number of competent drivers for such an event and that there are likely to be a number of sub-standard drivers operating as mobile hazards.

Two hours five minutes after the start Roger was called in by signals from Digger Digby's team at Mulsanne. Derek Ross refuelled the car with his usual expertise and the mechanics checked the oil. Alec Poole then took over for the difficult period that included nightfall. With four Lucas quartz halogen lamps putting 220 watts of light in the right places, the Sprite was as easy to drive as in daylight. The car ran the twenty-four hours with almost monotonous regularity, with a routine change of brake pads at the twelve hour mark. Conditions for the drivers were difficult with periods of rain and a wet track. Many competitors were put out by accidents and the yellow warning lights were on frequently.

At 3 pm Alec Poole crossed the line in fifteenth position overall, having covered 271 laps totalling 3650 kilometers (2268 miles), consuming 136 gallons of fuel at an average speed of 94·5 mph. Roger's fastest lap was 104 mph which, when compared with the 108 mph achieved in 1967, gives some idea of the effect of the track modification and wet conditions.

Poor Clive Baker had the clutch release mechanism jam on SR in the disengaged position after two hours, when he was due to make a pit stop. The clutch release sleeve had seized on the gearbox extension due to clutch dust from the sintered linings. Aubrey Woods of BRM later showed me how they had cured a similar problem by using dirt slots in the release sleeve, while Tuftriding the exterior. We later made this modification and eliminated the problem.

We were delighted with the Sprite's success and disappointed to lose the SR when it was going so well. At the celebration or unwinding dinner at our base, the Hotel du Croissant, Peter Browning made an odd speech that put a damper on proceedings. He announced to all the team and its supporters that this event was the last in which BMC would support the Healey efforts. Peter had obviously been instructed from above to tell us of this decision. So ended a long happy and fruitful era of collaboration in a year that had started with a grandiose competition programme.

This was the last time we ran a Sprite in a serious competition. From now on it was to be up to the private owners.

The Privateers

The large volume production of the Spridget, its suitability for racing and its low price resulted in a lot of activity from private entrants. Some were fortunate enough to get sponsorship or help from BMC, Austin, MG, the Donald Healey Motor Company, and various other companies associated with motoring. In common with several of the larger manufacturers, BMC operated a bonus scheme to encourage private entrants, rewarding those who achieved places in certain specified events. Quite a few team drivers also campaigned Sprites and Midgets privately, among them Alec Poole, John Harris, Mike Garton and Roger Enever.

Private owners had access to a considerable amount of tuning equipment from Warwick, Abingdon and a host of small firms, in addition to the excellent literature available on tuning the 'A' series engine. We supplied many owners with suspension modification parts, magnesium alloy wheels, exhaust systems and special braking kits. Other owners would go to independent tuners like Daniel Richmond and Les Rider, who could produce really worthwhile improvements to engine output. Paddy Hopkirk also supplied a lot of equipment, including steering wheels which had been used by us and BMC.

In the heyday of the Sprites, these activities kept Geoff Price pretty busy at Warwick. In this, he was fortunate to have the assistance of two men who were really conscientious workers. Derek Ross joined us after an apprenticeship at Austin–one of the best ways to learn; and Mike Dale, now a senior executive with British Leyland, spent some time working in our service department.

175

The Girling disc brake conversion we marketed for the Sprite. As a homologated extra these reliable Girling brakes did much to improve the cars' performance in competition.

Some of the more committed private entrants went to the expense of fitting their Spridget with a special body. Doug Wilson Spratt built a number of special coupé bodies in conjunction with Jim McManus. Known as WSMs, these were primarily road cars, being larger and heavier than our own specials. Special bodies were also available from John Sprinzel, who produced his own version of the Sebring Sprite. Onto the basic Sprite superstructure and centre section, he fitted a very neat, practical light alloy coupé body, built by Williams and Pritchard. These cars were distinctive, with nice lines.

John Sprinzel had a great deal of success campaigning these Sprites himself, particularly in rallies. He had cut his teeth competing with A35 saloons, and so the Sprite was a natural progression for him. He used Harry Weslake for a great deal of his engine tuning. In 1958 he came first in class in the Alpine Rally, while second and third places went to two other Sprite entries, driven by Tommy Wisdom and R. Brookes. In the 1959 Liège-Rome-Liège Rally, John and his co-driver Stuart Turner won the class and finished in twelfth position overall. In the 1960 RAC Rally, this time with Richard Bensted-

Doug Wilson Spratt built a number of special bodies on Sprites and 3000s. This Sprite, photographed in the paddock at Silverstone, was a very practical road car. (Alan Burman)

Alan Goodwin produced this lowered and lightened Sprite to make second fastest time of day at the Gaydon Sprint Meeting in 1968.

Doug Wilson-Spratt with the WSM Sprite-based car with which he completed the 1952 Monte Carlo Rally.

Smith as co-driver, he finished second overall and first in class. This private entry by John also won the *Autocar* Trophy, the *Autosport* Trophy, the BTRDA Trophy and the Hastings Trophy. Second place in the RAC Rally was to become a familiar position for the Big Healeys–Pat Moss and Ann Wisdom in 1961, Paddy Hopkirk in 1962, Timo Makinen in 1964 and 1965.

John also competed in the 1960 Liège-Rome-Liège, again winning the class and finishing in third position overall. This was probably the best ever Sprite rally result. Sprites were never great rally cars: their size, and the relatively small capacity of the engine meant that they simply did not have enough performance when carrying two people and heavy equipment over long and arduous courses. For a Sprite to cover the 3000 miles of the Liège-Rome-Liège, over rough roads at high speeds, demanded an exceptionally fit, tough driver.

John's decision to give his Sprites the name 'Sebring' gave the Warwick grumblers something to grumble about, as we had already registered the name with the Society of Motor Manufacturers and Traders. In fact, it was used by many other manufacturers as well and there was no real reason why he should not follow suit. He did race the cars at Sebring, and they did a lot of good for the marque's reputation. His 1961 effort with two Sprites at Sebring, described on page 127, was a private entry, receiving very little factory assistance. John also worked for us at Warwick, helping to set up the Healey Speed Equipment

Sebring 1961: Stirling Moss and Pat Moss passing the pits in John Sprinzel's Sebring Sprite. Pit Marshal John Baus in the foreground.

Division, which supplied tuning parts for private owners.

A number of special Midget GT coupé bodies were built by MG at Abingdon, and fitted on the Sprite/Midget platform chassis. A pair of these were campaigned to great effect by Dick Jacobs, an old MG driver. After a nasty accident at Le Mans in an MGA, Dick no longer raced, but his passion for racing was channelled into running a successful private team. Occasionally BMC's Competitions Department 'borrowed back' the cars for events like Sebring or the Targa Florio. Syd Enever had put considerable effort into the design and engineering of the bodies, and their aerodynamic qualities were second only to the Le Mans bodied Sprites.

A third team achieved quite memorable results in international events. This was the Sprite team run by Richard Groves of Claverdon. Richard and his driver, John Moore, an engineer with the Lockheed brake company, competed successfully in many club events with a rebuilt Sprite. John was often at Warwick in connection with the Borg and Beck clutches and the Lockheed brakes used on the Sprites and knew pretty well all that was going on. At the end of the 1964 season he knew that we were building new cars for 1965 and that the old ones would be for sale. He also knew that he would do better with one of these old cars as he had driven them during the course of brake development.

Progress was such that the previous year's cars could only be updated by means of a complete rebuild and we had decided that it would be better to start with a new chassis. Thus the old cars would have to be sold, either where they would do the most good or where they would make the most money. We rejected the second course as it was felt that the Sprite name might be damaged if the cars got into the possession of unruly idiots. They were fast and could be dangerous in the wrong hands. Richard Groves came over to Warwick and we discussed the possibility of his buying one of the cars, 693 LAC, with which Clive Baker had won the class in the Nassau races. The car was on a slow boat from the Bahamas and Richard agreed to come in and see it on its return. He duly came back with John and bought the car at a price lower than that of the production car, having first received my assurance that we would replace anything that was found to be worn.

John raced this car in a number of club events with good success. We then received a request from the German National Club, the Allgemeiner Deutscher Automobile Club, to run a car in the 1000 kilometre race at the Nürburgring, in May 1965, with an offer of good starting money. To have added the 1000 kilometre race to our racing programme at that time would have thrown everything out of order. We were fully committed and we might have lost one of the cars that was being prepared for the next event. I would have had to go over to run the car and I was not interested in visiting Germany. However, Stuart Turner at BMC had been asked to send a Midget and was keen that a Sprite ran as well, as Germany was an important market. DMH then asked

Richard Groves's ex Targa Florio Sprite and MG's GT version of the Midget at the Nürburgring. Richard raced Sprites on this circuit with much success.

me who was the best of the private owners and after much discussion we decided that Richard Groves and his Sprite fitted the bill. Richard had a good record and his cars were always a credit to the name.

I discussed the matter with Richard and after some hesitation and much encouragement from us he finally agreed to take over the entry, using his driver John Moore and our driver Clive Baker. He towed the car off to the Nürburgring behind his Austin Princess, while Clive followed with one of the ex-works Sebring 3000s. This car was to prove a useful practice machine with which the drivers took every opportunity to learn the 14 mile circuit. Clive had driven at the Nürburgring three times before and he was able to give John a lot of help in learning the course.

Richard ran the car with the aim of winning the class. His meticulous planning paid off and it came home first in the class, ahead of the Abarths, Renault Alpines and Alfa Romeos. Now bitten with the bug of international competition, Richard began expanding his involvement. After Le Mans we sold him the two Le Mans cars which he entered in the 1965 500 km race at the Nürburgring. As I anticipated, they put up an excellent performance, again winning their class ahead of the Abarth Fiats, Renault Alpines, Alfa Romeos, Midgets and Spitfires.

When DMH and Len Lord agreed on the production of the Austin Healey 100 in 1952, a competition programme followed naturally as a way of

The World Sprite expedition: without help from sponsors, Andrew Henderson (centre) and Neil Petrie (right) circumnavigated the world in a MkI Sprite. Chick Vandagriff, President of Hollywood Sports Cars Inc., came to the rescue when they suffered a blocked oil line after 50,000 miles.

Jerry Truitt campaigned this Sprite in the USA for Hank Thorp Inc, to become National Champion. Minilite wheels, renowned for their strength and accuracy, were often used on the works cars.

promoting the car. What is not generally known, however, is that we agreed that we would compete only in international events and mainly overseas, leaving the smaller events at home to private owners. We stuck to this rule rigidly, despite a number of inducements offered by race organizers. Only once did we depart from it and that was in 1963, at the behest of BMC's Competitions Department. At that time they were involved with Christobel Carlisle racing Minis, and wanted to extend this activity to include Sprites. We agreed to their proposals and Christobel drove one of our Sprites with Clive Baker at the 1963 Nürburgring 1000 Km. They finished with a very creditable seventeenth position overall, taking second place in class. After this, Christobel drove a Sprite in the BRDC Silverstone GT Race in May 1963. As she was coming through Woodcote, she got the back end too far out and crashed into the pits, fatally injuring an RAC official on duty at that point. Safety has since been greatly improved at most circuits and such an accident should not happen again, but after this episode we did not budge from our chosen line.

We used Silverstone a great deal to test and develop the competition cars. In the mid-sixties, when Stuart Turner was running the highly successful BMC Competitions Department, we co-operated at a number of test days in an attempt to select drivers. We took a racing Sprite and 3000 while Competitions produced various Minis and a works rally car. These selection trials were useful but could be misleading, as the competitive aspect of racing was absent. In long distance racing it is essential to obey the set limit for maximum engine

Richard Budd competing with the production version of the racing Sprite.

speed. As we were now using Smith's electronic tachometers without any maximum speed reading hand, we fitted additional mechanical rev counters in the engine compartment which enabled us to record the maximum speed used by the drivers without their knowledge. At every driver change I noted the reading and reset the instrument. A Sprite engine can be used to over 8000 rpm in a short distance event, but we were setting a limit of 6800 rpm which was what we would use in a long distance race.

In addition we had observers stationed all around the course, amongst them Ken Tyrell and Richard Groves, who would produce notes on the individual drivers. At the end of the day we had what we hoped was a reasonable assessment of the drivers' suitability. Stuart had great fun telling certain drivers about our secret recording devices. One driver who was dropped as a result of these tests later became highly successful in long-distance sports-car events, while one who was selected failed to measure up under the stress of racing. In all, however, the assessment of some fifteen drivers proved correct for thirteen, which cannot be considered too bad. As a result of these tests, Roger Enever and Alec Poole joined the team. Alec had previously prepared his own Sprite and was most impressed with the works cars.

With way over 100,000 Sprites and Midgets on the road, and the numerous club activities, it is impossible to do justice here to the many successful Spridget privateers. Today, one of the best special bodies available to private entrants is John Britten's Arkley SS. Reminiscent of pre-war designs, this is a distinctive and well made fibre-glass body, supplied as a kit. It can be fitted very easily and is especially popular with those owners who tire of their Sprite's or Midget's appearance.

Finding
and
Fixing

Finding and restoring an old car is always a chancy business, as even after most careful examination, removal of body panels may reveal severe hidden rot. Restoration work is expensive and one has to consider carefully what one pays for a car and what the anticipated expenditure on restoration is likely to be. Some cars will be so far gone that it will sometimes be impossible to produce a satisfactory end product.

Cars can be found in a variety of places. Owen Swinnerd found a Sprite in running order abandoned by the roadside, and about to be towed away by the police. He located the owner and bought it for £1, having first persuaded the police not to impound it. Deryk Walker of the St Albans Sprite group bought one for £7. Both are now committed to some hard restoration work.

One cannot restore old cars without spare parts and in this respect Austin Healey cars are better supplied than most, by Fred Draper of A. H. Spares, Tachbrook Road, Leamington Spa. Fred ran the stores at the old Cape factory and gained an early insight into obtaining parts when the illness of the purchasing director made it necessary for him to do most of the buying, in addition to the spares supply work. When this director retired due to ill health, Fred carried on this work with Gordon Barton.

When our relations with BLMC soured, the Donald Healey Motor Co. gave up the Austin franchise and instead took on FIAT. Although FIAT is one of the better foreign cars, Fred decided he would like to leave, to continue selling Austin Healey parts independently. The stores were loaded with a vast quantity of spares going back to the 1953 models, including many of the special parts like light alloy panels, cylinder heads and gaskets of every description. All the spare parts, lists and spares records were sold to Fred who then set up shop in Royal Leamington Spa.

One would have expected a declining spares market, if the cars had gradually faded away like most models. Instead Fred has found an ever increasing demand and has even had to have some old parts tooled up and re-manufactured. He is now selling more spares than he ever did at Warwick, to far more satisfied customers.

One should be very careful in the selection of who is entrusted with restoration work. Such work is not cheap and there are many pitfalls for the unwary or the unlucky. Even worse than poor workmanship is the loss of the car. One unfortunate friend lost his in a fire in the restorer's workshop, where the owner of the shop was not insured and only took work in at owner's risk. Before entrusting your car to a restorer, do make certain that it is covered by insurance. This cover is nothing like as expensive as the normal road risks policy. Another unfortunate paid part of the costs in advance: the restorer then stripped the car and used the parts on other rebuilds before going out of business. Don't be misled by flamboyant advertisements: ask around before taking a risk. The various clubs have a good idea of who is competent and trustworthy. Although they cannot publish warnings about particular restorers who are known to be crooked or about to go bust, knowledgeable members may be persuaded to give sound advice.

Most Frog-eye owners try to restore all its original characteristics. The appearance of the car has become one of its many endearing features, and indeed you will only devalue it by rebodying it, fitting spurious parts, or even improving it. When *Drive*, the Automobile Association's useful magazine, was introduced, I was invited to join a panel together with Harry Webster of Triumph, to give my views on what would be the next 'classic' car. Harry naturally chose a Triumph product – the razor-edged Renown, while I had no hesitation in choosing the original Sprite. I think that most people would agree that the MkI does not deserve to have its bodywork removed, although the same is not necessarily true of the MkII and later versions.

Fibreglass, or glass-reinforced plastic, has been looked on with scorn by the purists. While it is true that some of the earlier GRP panels were very poor in shape and finish, the quality has since improved and many GRP parts are now quite acceptable. In addition, of course, the use of GRP does reduce the incidence of corrosion, one of the problems with cars built in the fifties and sixties. With the exhorbitant price of original steel parts, not many people can afford to be purists today and it is surely right to use this material to make a high quality restoration at considerably lower cost.

John Britten of John Britten Garages Ltd. has come up with an original solution to the problem, producing an attractively styled sports car based on the Spridget understructure. Owners of Spridgets with sound understructures, who want to revamp the body, would be well advised to buy one of his conversion kits. The price is very reasonable—in the region of £125, and the work involved is relatively simple.

The use of high quality body steel for Sprite and Midget panels, and the excellence of the BMC paint process at the Morris plant in Cowley, gave the cars a high degree of rust resistance. Both BMC and the Pressed Steel Co. imported body steel from the United States, where the quality was far superior to anything produced in Europe. This material has wonderful drawing qualities, having been produced to meet the exacting demands of the US automobile industry, with a surface finish that helps paint adhesion. Unfortunately, accident damage and subsequent body shop repairs often result in a reduction in corrosion resistance.

There are a great variety of paints and primers available to retard corrosion of steel parts. Steel starts to rust very quickly in a humid atmosphere. Once rust has formed it encourages further rusting as it is hygroscopic and attracts more moisture. Some means of protection can be afforded to steel by a phosphoric acid wash, or a coating of a zinc rich paint. On top of this a coating of some form of undersealing compound gives the best underbody protection.

We are inclined to look back and remember that corrosion was not a problem in the fifties and sixties. Although this was to a large extent true of the Spridget, my files show that we received quite a few complaints about paint finish and durability on the 100 and 3000 series. A number of different treatments were tried, but it was not until later on that the source of the problem was diagnosed as galvanic action between the different metals at the wing joint—the area where paint adhesion was most prone to failure. Of the three types of metal used—the aluminium for the skin panels, the mild steel for the understructure, and the stainless steel for the beading and clips, the aluminium, being the less noble metal, suffered the worst.

To prevent corrosion of aluminium it is necessary to take great care to achieve and maintain a non-porous coating. Otherwise a greatly accelerated attack may be concentrated at the imperfections in the coating. The use of a zinc chromate primer on the joint faces and dipping the fixing screws in zinc chromate is recommended. Some additional protection can be obtained by using Densochrome tape or Duralac between these joints. This type of corrosion can be severe where salt is used on roads in winter. Washing down with soft water under the wings helps slow the process. There are a variety of special oils that can be sprayed underneath the wings and on the chassis, while the dewatering fluids will remove water and provide limited protection. Every day new compounds are coming onto the market. Cars that suffer from oil leaks usually benefit from reduced corrosion: oil is an excellent protector of metal.

The MkI Sprites and MkII/MkI Spridgets, with their quarter elliptic springs, feed very high loads into the spring mounting point in the body. This point is subject to spray from the wheels and it is advisable to inspect and clean it thoroughly and regularly. If any repair work is necessary, it should then be well coated with preservative.

The front lower suspension trunnions of the MksI-III are liable to seize up, due to failure to lubricate properly. Here again, these trunnions should be stripped and cleaned regularly. If left unattended, the swivel pin trunnion and lower wishbone may have to be replaced. Frequent greasing with a grease containing molybdenum disulphide is recommended.

Armstrong have always recommended that only their special damper oil should be used in the shock absorbers. However, on many a racing car this was drained off and replaced by SAE30 engine oil or even Castrol R40 to make the damping more effective – and it did seem to work. With worn engines that are using oil, it is often better and more economical to use a suitable grade of engine oil, changing the viscosity to suit the temperature conditions, as recommended in the handbook. A 40 weight oil is more effective than an IOW40 oil at maintaining pressure where outside temperatures are in the 90 degree F range. It is also quite satisfactory down to 55 degree ambient. We invariably raced on single grade oils, using Castrol's R40 castor-base oil on the Sprite. Castor base oil is not really suitable for normal motoring, however.

Spridget owners who intend to race their cars should pay special attention to the rear axle. This was always a problem area with our racing cars. The actual crown wheel or ring gear and pinion were well designed and well made and gave us no trouble at all. After each race, these components would always be in excellent condition – and some crown wheel and pinion sets were in race service for a long time.

The problems existed at the axle ends. The effects of increased engine power and increased tyre adhesion with Dunlop's excellent racing tyres were marked. After each race we would strip and examine many of the component parts to see if they were suitable for further use. Early axle shafts showed evidence of twisting at the inner splined ends but this trouble disappeared when shafts of higher tensile strength were introduced. However, we then found that the bearings were coming loose on the axle tube ends. Originally the axle tube ends had right-hand threads at each end; these were changed early in the production life to one left-hand and one right-hand, thereby eliminating any chance of a nut undoing and the consequent loss of a wheel assembly.

A minimum of improvement was made by machining hubs of heavier section in a better grade of steel. This did little to improve the loosening of the bearing on the axle tube although since the axle ends were of the semi floating type, axle shaft failure could no longer result in the disastrous loss of a wheel. With the designed output and loadings of the A35 and Sprite in normal form, the axles were more than adequately strong. However there was no room available in the design to increase the size of the axle shaft, tube end or nut.

For years we got away with using higher tensile axle shafts and a new axle casing for each race. The assembly of the bearings to the tube end was critical. Each time a bearing was fitted and removed, the fit of the bearing on the axle tube end became looser. To obtain the best results nuts were done up tight by feel: too much force would stretch the threads, too little would cause the bearing to become slack. This was and still remains an area where the greatest care in assembly pays dividends.

On the last cars George Delaselle, BMC's great transmission specialist, arranged the supply of axle cases with ends made in a high tensile steel. With these, coupled with careful assembly using Loctite bearing retaining adhesive, the problem was licked. The nuts were always locked with the production tab washer and it was important to carry out the locking operation carefully to avoid loosening the nut. Careful assembly of the axle ends using close fitting nuts, Loctite and the special BMC octagonal spanner will be rewarded by trouble free life.

A perennial problem on all cars when under racing conditions is the weight transfer from the inner to the outer wheel in a corner, causing a lack of traction due to the tendency for the inner wheel to lift and spin. To overcome this, limited slip differentials are used. One of the best known for use with the Sprite is the ZF, a German device developed by Zahnradfabrik Friedrichshafen in 1931. This stemmed from the differential incorporated in the wartime military version of the Volkswagon, patented by Gottfried Weidmann. Although reliable, the ZF is somewhat rough in operation and was always expensive throughout the period of its production.

BMC and other companies developed limited slip differentials that were sweeter in action and consequently preferred by racing drivers. However, in their design the space available for the differential pinions was reduced and gears of a weaker tooth form had to be fitted. Although exhaustive testing did not reveal any problems, the pinions lasted a very short time under actual race conditions. For this reason, we reverted to the ZF device for later racing Sprites, although we were always very keen to use in-house products. We had hoped that the day would come when they would be fitted to production cars, to the benefit of private owners, but unfortunately this never materialized. I would still recommend Spridget owners to fit ZFs for racing; to the best of my knowledge, they are fairly easy to obtain second-hand.

One of the penalties of having one's own name on a marque is that one is often pestered by people who delude themselves into thinking that they have discovered a valuable old car. Research in this area is difficult and often fruitless: one usually finds that the car in question is a very ordinary production model of no special significance.

BN1L 133235. One of the first Austin Healeys built and used by DMH on his 1953 tour of USA. Donald G. Paye found it in this delapidated barn near New York. It is now in the process of restoration.

Very occasionally, however, one of the very special cars will come to light in this way. Such was the case on 8th November 1977, when I opened a letter from Donald Paye of Greenfield, Massachusetts, giving a mass of details of a 1953 Austin Healey 100 with the chassis number 133235. This number interested me, for it struck a chord in my memory. I searched through my dog-eared oil-stained notebooks and there it was, on page 22 of the experimental chassis records: AHX3 BN1L133235. This meant that it was one of the first four 100s ever built, the first three of which were shipped over on one of the *Queens* from Southampton to New York. Interestingly, it was also noted as having had a 500 m road test. This meant that DMH and I had run it down to Perranporth and back, our usual procedure with a car we were going to put to some serious use. I finally came to the conclusion that this was the car DMH had used on his sales tour of the USA, covering some 10,000 miles including a demonstration run at Sebring on 8th March. I later found more records confirming this fact.

The likelihood of one of our special works Sprites being discovered in a similar way is unfortunately even more remote, because of the sheer number of Spridgets produced. As on the Big Healeys, we fixed our Donald Healey Motor Company identification plates to all the works competition cars. The Targa Florio cars were given a TFR number in the space marked 'Type', while most of the others had an ST or special test number. This refers to the specification which was drawn up at the time of manufacture. Morris Engines fitted plates bearing raised letters and figures, beginning XSP, to all the special engines. In addition, the Le Mans engines had an RAC stamp added to the plate.

I have supplied the clubs with a great deal of information on the works cars, taken from the files which we drew up for every race car and every event. It is well worth joining a club simply to take advantage of the wealth of information they are continually collecting. Do remember, however, that it is a simple matter for a skilled mechanic to change the engine and chassis plates from one car to another. The original number of a genuine works Sprite, registration at present in America, has also been found on another Sprite in the UK!

The Clubs

Spridget owners today are well served by the network of Austin Healey and MG clubs which literally span the globe. The MG Car Club naturally has the longest pedigree, having been formed in 1930. Its first secretary was John Thornley, who joined MG's service department at Abingdon in 1931. John put a really tremendous effort into his various activities–running the MG factory, guiding the clubs, preaching the cult of the sports car, stimulating MG's sports car magazine, *Safety Fast*, and writing a history of the MG marque, *Maintaining the Breed*, which has since become a classic.

The very first Healey club, known as the Healey Drivers Club, was formed in 1955 and operated in a very free and easy manner. Numerous small groups grew up around the world, catering for both Big Healey and Sprite owners. The first club specifically devoted to Sprite owners was the Southern Counties Sprite Club, which was formed in 1959 and had over 400 members within only two years. This promoted a very lively competition and social programme and under Raymond Baxter and Doug Worgan gave its members a lot of fun.

In 1961, primarily at the suggestion of John Thornley, the Austin Healey Club Ltd. was formed, as the proprietor of all these small groups. Many of them needed quite a lot of persuading that it was in their interests to come under the same banner, but Brian Healey, Peter Browning and John Thornley eventually convinced them. John used the MG Car Club as the model on which

World champion Bruce McLaren with a Sprite and John Cooper with one of his racing cars. John used the BMC 'A' series engine in the Mini Cooper S and in his formula Junior racing cars. (Austin Morris)

The current MGB and Midget. (Austin Morris)

The MG Car Club and the Austin Healey Club shared a stand at the 1965 Racing Car Show, displaying the 1965 Le Mans MGB and Sprite. Peter Browning did a tremendous job organizing the AHC and was its first general secretary.

to base the organization of the new club, which was also based at Abingdon. BMC provided secretarial services and back-up, and *Safety Fast* gave equal space to Austin Healeys and MGs, its cover giving pride of place to each marque alternately.

In 1967, the heyday of BMC sports production and club activities, a joint race meeting was organized at Silverstone by both clubs. Unfortunately, subsequent reorganization following the formation of BLMC meant that the Austin Healey Club was pushed out of Abingdon, and co-operation between the two clubs on a formal level has since declined. Ironically, although membership was high during the BMC days, application forms being sent out with all new cars, the interest shown by members is probably far greater today than ever before.

Despite the Austin Healey name dropping from production, club activities are increasing all the time and in fact recent meets have been over-subscribed. In Britain, the Midland Centre organizes many of the national meetings. On 14th May 1978, they arranged a Jubilee Forum at Warwick to celebrate the 25th anniversary of the start of Healey production at Austin. In addition to some well preserved cars, several well preserved motor men also turned out for this event, including Doc Weaving, Gil Jones and Wally Hassan. The final driving test for a magnificent trophy donated by Lucas was won by Paul Weston and his Sprite. The Midland Centre also organized an International

Margot presenting the Lucas Trophy to Paul Weston, the owner of a concours Sprite that has won many driving tests.

Brother Brian sent his immaculate Frog-eye to the Jubilee Forum, driven by his son Peter, as he was busy opening his new Wine Bar at Perranporth.

Alan Zafer and DMH at the Austin Healey Jubilee Forum.

Healey Day at Weston Park on 9th July 1978. DMH came up from Cornwall to present the prizes, while Geoff Price estimated that around 500 Big Healeys and Sprites and over 1000 people joined in the activities. Chairman Phil Wilkes and social secretary Carolyn Walters can be justifiably proud of their organization and the great pleasure it brings to so many.

Over in the USA, the Austin Healey Club of America was formed in March 1961 with Chuck Anderson as regional director, which establishes it as one of the oldest of the Austin Healey Clubs. In late 1962 the Club became affiliated to the main Austin Healey Club, after some persuasion from Peter Browning. Like all the clubs, it suffered when first the Big Healey and then the Sprite were dropped from production, and when the newly formed BLMC decided to withdraw its support. Some US clubs disappeared, but others, like the Austin Healey Club of America, adapted to deal with the situation. In 1975, under Walt Blanck's leadership, and with his genius for organization, the club became formally dedicated to the preservation of the marque through restoration, and began redeveloping area groups to cope with the vast distances between the various centres. These area clubs have continued to grow, and by the start of 1978 total membership exceeded 1000.

Walt Blanck was responsible for organizing the first National Conclave, which was held in Bloomington, Indiana in July 1976. This has since become

Chuck Anderson, with the Big Healey shirt, assists with an interview at the Austin Healey Club of America's 1978 Conclave. The police departement, who provided such splendid protection for the valuable cars, also made a video tape recording of the proceedings.

an annual event, the second being held in the Allegheny Mountains at Seven Springs Resort, near Champion, Pennsylvania, and the third, in 1978, at Louisville, Kentucky. DMH was invited to attend this event, but as he had not fully recovered from a recent operation to replace a hip joint, he felt he would not be able to do it justice. Walt Blanck then asked me to stand in for him. I was delighted to accept, especially as I had not been to the USA since our last Sebring race of 1968. Organization and systems are a great part of American life and were displayed to great effect throughout the Conclave. The events included a concourse, a rally, a gymkhana and an awards banquet. I handed over a number of excellent trophies and awards, including one to Mike Callahan of Ohio for the best Healey in the world (with subsequent protestations from some of my English friends!), and in turn received the first of the plaques produced by the Austin Healey Club of America to commemorate the 25th anniversary of the Austin Healey. I was also presented with Honorary Citizenship Certificates for DMH and myself by the Deputy Mayor of Louisville, and was in addition made a Kentucky Colonel. I was surprised and a little shattered at this unexpected award.

One particularly interesting feature of the conclave was a series of informal technical sessions, where I answered owners' questions and helped them sort out some obscure problems. I was delighted to explain some of the old wrinkles used to cure overdrive faults. Many of the cars taking part had been restored to a very high standard, which would put many of their British counterparts to shame, while a good proportion were still used as everyday transport, with

The Austin Healey Club of America produced this plaque to mark the 25th anniversary of the marque. Beautifully produced and individually numbered, these will become collectors' pieces.

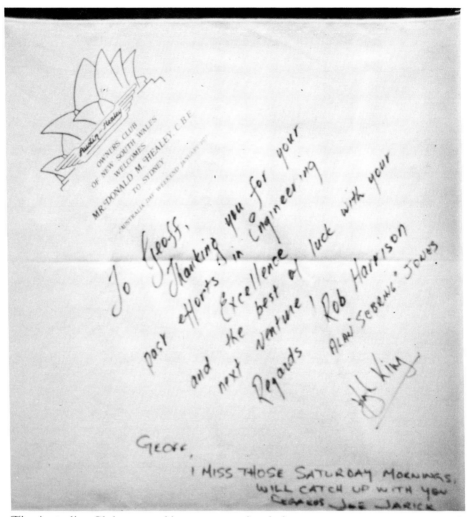

The Australian Club sent us this commemorative cloth.

100,000 miles plus on the clock. After the conclave, I flew on to Detroit to see some more Healeys, including Gary Kohs's 1965 Sebring Sprite. This was the first of the streamlined coupés to be used in the last years at Le Mans. Gary first saw the car at Sebring in 1965 and decided then and there that he would own it one day. It has an enviable race record, having finished some 34 long-distance races.

In the past, I had little to do with the clubs, as I was so heavily involved with design, development and competition. Knowing so many secrets, I sometimes felt awkward when particularly acute questions were asked by knowledgeable members, and most of the liaison work between the company and the clubs was undertaken by my brother Brian, one time general secretary, and by Geoff Price. Now that the cars are no longer in production, all this has changed. I find that I don't really need to own a Healey, as I can instead enjoy the many cars which have been so lovingly restored and maintained throughout the world.

The listing given below is intended to help owners or people interested in Austin Healeys or MGs make contact with their fellow enthusiasts. It should be stressed that the clubs do not provide a meeting place for bigoted purists, but for all sports car enthusiasts. One prominent MG Car Club member recently sought my advice about restoring one of the last of the Le Mans Sprites, while quite a few Austin Healey Club members own MGs and even Jaguars. Nowadays, club membership is almost essential for anyone who wants to gain information about the cars, locate difficult spare parts or obtain advice on any aspect of restoration.

Austin Healey Clubs

Australia

Austin Healey Sprite Drivers Club, PO Box 248, Box Hill, Victoria 3128. President: Alex Robinson.

Austin Healey Owners Club of New South Wales, GPO Box 2628, Sydney 2001. President: Alan 'Sebring' Jones.

Southern Australian Austin Healey Owners Club, 24 Monalta Dr, Belair, South Australia 5052. President: John Read.

Austin Healey Owners Club of Victoria, 18 Brendales Ave, Blackburn, Victoria 3130. President: Roger Rayson.

Austin Healey Owners Club of Queensland, 17 Morehead Ave, Norman Park, Queensland 4170. President: Carl Stecher.

Canada

Calgary Austin Healey Club, MPO Box 2293, Calgary, Alberta T2P 2M6. President: Ken Barrow.

Austin Healey Owners Association of British Columbia, PO Box 80274, South Burnaby, BC, V5H 3X5. President: John Swann.

Austin Healey Club of America: Toronto region: Ed DeLong, 2959 Nipiwin Dr, Mississauga, Ont.
Hamilton region: Rich Chrysler, 96 Charlotte St, Hamilton, Ont. L8K 4V2.

Europe

Austria: Franz Aigner, A-1200 Wien, Plankenmaisstrasse 20, Austria.

Austin Healey Club of Denmark, Morgans Rosenkilde, Rormosevej 20, 2400 NV, Copenhagen, Denmark.

Germany: Peter Kuprianoff, Leopoldstrasse 24A, 7500 Karlsruhe, W. Germany.

Austin Healey Owners Club Nederlands, J. P. Broers, De Gondel 15, Baarn, Holland.
Austin Healey Club of Sweden, Keneth Andren, Loviselundsvagen 34, 162–35 Vallingby, Sweden.
Austin Healey Club Schweiz, Felix Gugola, Veberlandstrasse 199A, 8600 Dubendorf, Switzerland.

Great Britain
Midland Centre: Mel Knight, 17 Glebe Rd, Groby, Leics.
South-Western Centre: Mrs Carol Marks, 171 Coldharbour Rd, Bristol BS6 7SX.
Eastern Centre: David Hicks, 102 Fairfax Dr, Westcliff-on-Sea, Essex.
New Forest Centre: Mrs Pat Martin, 104 Winchester Rd, Shirley, Southampton, Hants.
Southern Counties: Mike Allman, 28 Strathearn Ave, Whitton, Middx.
Southern Counties: Phil Wakefield, 99 Bourneside Rd, Addlestone, Surrey.
Thames Valley Centre: Tom Oakman, 14 Burnt Oak Rd, Wokingham, Berks.
Northern Centre: Sheila Reich, 61 Winstanley Rd, Sale, Cheshire M33 2AG.
St Albans Group: Derek Walker, 16 Folley Ave, St Albans, Herefordshire.

New Zealand
Austin Healey Car Club of New Zealand Inc, PO Box 25–016, St Heliers, Auckland 5, President: Mark Donaldson.

Southern Africa
Austin Healey Club of Southern Africa, Ron Field, PO Box 68399, Bryanston, Transvaal.

United States of America
Austin Healey Club of America, 705 Dimmeydale Rd, Deerfield, Il 60015. President: Walter H. Blanck Jr.
Regional directors:
Chicago, Il: Gary Brierton, 330 Ash Park Forest, Il 60466.
Detroit, Mi: Gary Dewey, 1972 Maryland, Birmingham, Mi 48009.
Indianapolis, In: Jon Silverberg, 8413 E 82nd St, Indianapolis, In 46256.
Charlotte, NC: Russell Jenkins III, Rt 9, Box 564, Monroe, NC 28110.
Dayton, Oh: Dale Beal, 1210 Richar St, Miamisburg, Oh 45342.
Ft Wayne, In: James R. White, 427 Arcadia Ct, Ft Wayne, In 46807.
Columbus, Oh: Pat Thackery, 904 South Roosevelt, Bexley, Oh 43209.
Louisville, Ky: Howell Moore, Jr, 3327 Stratford Ave, Louisville, KY 40218.
DC, Maryland, Virginia: David Doyle, 12806 Valleywood Dr, Wheaton, Md 20906.
Cleveland/Akron, Ohio: Mike Callahan, 556 Wooster St, Canal Fulton, Oh 44614.
New England: Don Paye, 1207 Barnardston Rd, Greenfield, Ma 01301.
Virginia: Doug Mckay, Virginia Beach, Va.
Austin Healey Club, Pacific Centre, PO Box 6267, San Jose, Ca 95150. President: Lou Buch.
Austin Healey Club of South California, PO Box 4082, Riverside, Ca 92514. President: Jim Mayfield.

Austin Healey Club of Oregon, 3102 SE 7th Portland, Oregon 97202.
Austin Healey Club of Hawaii, 1508 Al Keeaumoru St, Honolulu 5, Hawaii. President:
  Rodney Hudik.

MG Clubs

Australia

Gold Coast Centre: Valda Thompson, PO Box 103, Surfers Paradise, Queensland
  4217.
New South Wales Centre: Frank Bett, PO Box 5165, GPO, Sydney 2001.
Newcastle Centre: PO Box 62A, Newcastle, NSW 2300.
MG Car Club of Western Australia Inc: Vic Longden, PO Box U1924, GPO, Perth,
  Western Australia 6001.

Canada

Canadian Classic: Harold Lunner, PO Box 48452, PS Bentall Centre, Vancouver, BC
  V7X IA2.

Europe

Belgium MG Car Club: Pierard Franz, 37 Rue Delvaux, 6040 Jumet, Belgium.
Danish Centre: Svend Carstensen, Genuavej 45, 2300 Kbhvn S, Denmark.
Danish Centre West: Poul H. Jensen, PO Box 6, 6330 Padborg, DK, Denmark.
Frankfurt Centre: Gisela Dessau, Postfach 442, D6370, Oberursel, W. Germany.
MG Car Club Holland: W van der Veer, JF Kennedyplantsoen 54 Voorschoten,
  Holland.
Italian Centre: F Filipello, Via Vetulonia 38/A, 00183 Rome, Italy.
Luxembourg Centre: Ton Maathuis, 1 Rue Tomm, Fouhren, Luxembourg.
Norwegian Centre: John Erik Skjefstad, Kastanjeveien 19, Oslo 4, Norway.
MG Car Club of Sweden: Lennarth Gustafson, Vardshusvagen 6, 17173 Huddinge,
  Sweden.
MG Car Club of Switzerland: Arnold Flammer, Burggraben 24, CH-9000 St Gallen,
  Switzerland.
Dalmatia Centre: Slobodan Jelich, 58000 Split, Hektorvicca 34, Yugoslavia.

Great Britain

MG Car Club Ltd: General Secretary, Gordon Cobban, PO Box 126, Brentwood,
  Essex CM15 8RP.
South-Eastern Centre: Peter Faulks, Devonshire Cottage, Dynes Hall Rd, Gt Maple-
  stead, Halstead, Essex.
South-Western Centre: Mike Hawk, 117 Upper Westwood, Bradford-on-Avon, BA15
  2DN.
Devon and Cornwall Centre: RG-Slatter, 170 Vicarage Gdns, St Budeaux, Plymouth,
  Devon.
Midland Centre: D. Whale, 22 Sandford Close, Hill Ridware, Rugeley, Staffs.
North-Western Centre: J. Cocker, 3 Bollin Dr, Brooklands Rd, Sale, Cheshire.
North-Eastern Centre: R. Drake, 8 Mount Ave, Wrenthorpe, Wakefield.
Lincolnshire Sub-centre: John Laurence, 36 St Margaret's Dr, Sibsey, Boston, Lincs.
Tyne-Tees Centre: AW Wood, Ham Hall, Scruton, Northallerton, North Yorks.

Scottish Centre: Douglas Nickel, 12 N St Andrew St, Edinburgh EH2 1HT.
Ulster Centre: Michael Wilson, Summerseat, Marino, Holywood, Co. Down.

Japan
MG Car Club, Japan Centre: Y Kuboyama, 5–8–605, Kitamachi 3-Chome, Kichi-joji, Musashino-shi, Tokyo 180, Japan.

New Zealand
Auckland Centre: CM Grant, PO Box 6483, Auckland 1.

Southern Africa
MG Car Club, Johannesburg Centre: Mrs M. Nunn, PO Box 52336, Saxonwold 2132, Transvaal.
MG Car Club, Cape Town Centre: PO Box 2808, Cape Town.
Natal Centre: Hedley M. Adams, PO Box 10260, Marine Parade, 4056.
Port Elizabeth Centre: 39 York Rd, North End, Port Elizabeth.
MG Car Club, Northern Transvaal Centre: PO Box 17006, Groenkloof, 0027 Pretoria.

United States of America
Southern Connecticut MGCC: David F. Raymond, Clover Leaf Shell, Main & Glover Aves, Norwalk, Conn 06850.
North West Center: Mrs Nikki Daniels, 11232 312th NE, Carnation, Washington 98014.
Southwestern Ohio Center: Mrs A. Urick, 1966 East Stroop Rd, Dayton, Oh 45429.
Rocky Mountain Center: Mrs Arlene Chapman, 8071 Ivy St, Box No 4, Dupont, Col 80024.
Eastgate Dunes MGCC: Mrs Ginny Crane, PO Box 60, Allenhurst, NJ 07711.
MG Owners' Association, Central Jersey Center: Kathleen G. Hennessy, 20 North Mapel Ave, Basking Ridge, NJ 07920.
Houston MGCC: Brian Daly, 5711 Winding Creek, Houston, Texas 77009.
St Louis Center: Miss Janette Myles, 2034 Brown Rd, Overland, St Louis, Mo 63114.
Louisiana Center: E. E. Reynolds, PO Box 2112, Reserve, La 70084.
Long Beach MGCC: Diane Pridgeon, PO Box 1727, Long Beach, Ca 90801.
Abingdon Rough Riders: Allan J. Chalmers, 1231 12th Ave, San Francisco, Ca 94122.
New England Center: Barbara B. Stasiak, 69 Jacques St, Somerville, Mass 02145.
Washington DC Center: Mike Hughes, 6609 N. Benson Dr, Alexandria, Va 22306.
Lake Erie Center: J. Rosseger, 15719 Chadbourne Rd, Shaker Heights, Oh 44120.
Florida Center: William R. McQuaid, 1419 Seaboard Coast Line Bldg, Jacksonville, Fla 32202.
San Diego Center: Larry Gibson, 924 Spinel Ave, El Cajon, Ca 92021.
Northern California Center: Mrs Helen Corbett, 20 Yankee Hill, Oakland, Ca 94618.
Western New York Center: Michael Gaglio, 263 Beechwood Cres, Webster, NY 14580.
Long Island Center: Mernu M. Lehmann, 256 Riviera Dr, Smithtown, NY 11787.

An Age of Change

Apart from a handful of prototypes and about twenty competition vehicles, all the Sprites and Midgets were produced by the MG Car Company at Abingdon. John Thompson Motor Pressings built the chassis understructures onto which Pressed Steel Company assembled the bodies, but each subsequent stage of the production process was carried out by a member of the BMC group, under the control of MG. Overall production engineering, scheduling, procurement of materials and quality control were all the ultimate responsibility of MG. In the past, Jensen may have tended to give the impression that they manufactured all the Healey cars. In fact, although Jensen built and finished the bodies of the Big Healeys, they had virtually no involvement with the Sprites or Midgets.

Since its foundation by Cecil Kimber, MG had always retained the atmosphere of a family firm, despite two major upheavals: firstly when the company was bought by Morris Motors of Cowley in 1935, and secondly when Morris in turn merged with Austin to form the British Motor Corporation in 1952. After Cecil Kimber's tragic death in a railway accident, MG was to enjoy the single-minded management of John Thornley, who first joined the company in 1931. He was responsible for building up MG as the sports car division of BMC and in this was supported by a very skilled and loyal staff, most of whom spent most of their working days with the company. John was able to generate a great sense of pride and team spirit amongst his workforce—both for the name of MG and for all the cars the company produced. His chief engineer, Syd Enever, had a great bunch of men working under him, including Roy Brockle-

A club visit to the MG factory, with a line up of their range of sports cars. The MG record breaker is in the foreground.

hurst, Jim O'Neill, Terry Mitchel, Don Hayter, Alec Hounslow, Jerry Stone and Tom Haig, while the efficient production team included men such as Les Lambourn, Cecil Cousins, Charlie Martin and Reg Jackson.

Some Americans may consider Tupelo the centre of the Universe, but MG was certainly the centre of the world's sports car production. In the late 1960s, MG's share of the world market was virtually unchallenged, with an output of no less than six different sports models, ranging from the Sprite to the Austin Healey 3000.

When the production of Austin Healeys was transferred from Austin to MG in 1956, DMH and I had some initial misgivings. We had a great respect for Austin and at that time had not had much experience of working with MG. John Thornley called us down to Abingdon to assure us that his company would do as well as if not better than Austin, and these assurances were to be borne out by MG's performance. Often, when a company takes over a design, it treats it with a 'not invented here' attitude, sometimes going to extremes to prove it to be inferior to its own creations. This was never the case with MG. Syd Enever and his men did everything possible to improve the various Healey marques they produced, no doubt spurred on by the challenge to turn out a better product than had Austin with their much larger facilities. Many people in authority at BMC did not quite understand what made MG tick, and some would have liked to have moved the whole operation over to a factory with larger production lines, in the interest of production efficiency. Then as now, there was a lot of squawking to the effect that the lack of investment in the motor industry was responsible for poor performance. But it is the men that make good motor cars and not the machines, and MG did wonders with their old factory and a minimum of equipment. In fact, a thorough investigation revealed that MG were producing vehicles as efficiently as any other part of the group.

Only three people at the Donald Healey Motor Company at Warwick had close contact with MG and BMC–DMH, my brother Brian and myself. DMH was the ideas man, thinking up new cars which were then left to me to design and execute in metal. Brian was mainly interested in the marketing

Under the bonnet of an MG Midget. This shows the high standard of finish typical of all MG products.

1962: the first coupé body we built on a Sprite chassis, photographed at the old Cape works. DMH's office is to the right of the double doors, with the drawing office windows above.

aspects, dealing with the Motor Show, public relations and club activities. The close co-operation between BMC and our own company intensified the need for commercial and technical secrecy and it was thus essential that none of BMC's or our own secrets were leaked from Warwick. Customers and the sales and service staffs from directors downwards were excluded from our experimental workshop and the design office. We worked under great pressure and unnecessary interruptions from other departments had to be avoided. This caused some friction when members of our staff observed the free access given to our friends at BMC, Lucas, Girling and Dunlop, who were privy to so many secrets. As a result, anyone attempting to build up a story of the Healey cars by questioning people outside the three of us would tend to be given a distorted picture.

We were frequent visitors to MG and were always made welcome. Warwick and Abingdon are only 60 miles apart, linked by a very pleasant route over the

The Monte Carlo Rally Sprite in the dispatch park at Abingdon, with USA-bound Sprites waiting for boats. Shipping caused a bottle-neck at times.

Cotswolds, and we would often drive over to get Syd's expert opinion on some engineering detail. Syd had a characteristic pose when considering a problem, crouching down on his haunches. Naturally, anyone else involved in the discussion would be forced to do likewise, to the amusement of curious onlookers.

As a result of good management, stringent quality control and thorough road testing, the cars delivered from MG to dealers required very little in the way of pre-delivery inspection before handing over to the customer. In fact some garages merely screwed on the registration plates and stuck their adhesive label on the rear window. These labels often reacted with the clear Vyback, making a nasty mark and requiring the whole hood to be replaced! Faults were found early and cured immediately, although improvements took a little longer to incorporate. Small or relatively small volume producers have an advantage in being able to react quickly in an emergency.

I remember that on one occasion, a delivery driver brought a new Sprite up to Warwick from MG, complaining of a slipping clutch. I tried the car and found that the clutch was indeed slipping, and that the brakes were also binding. In checking it over, I noticed a characteristic sheen of mineral oil in the combined hydraulic brake and clutch reservoir. I rang Syd Enever and told him about it and within the hour he was back on the phone with the explanation and cure. The assembly line drew its supplies of hydraulic brake fluid from a large tank and this tank was subject to routine quality checks.

The assembly line at Abingdon, with a MkII Sprite on the left and an MG Midget on the right. Quality cars are made on this type of track and pushed along by the workforce.

However, between checks, mineral oil had somehow found its way into the tank to cause contamination on a number of cars. Due to the production control laid down by MG and their speed of reaction, this fault was narrowed down to a small number of cars, including a number at the factory and on the line. The same day all garages having these suspect cars were notified of the fault and given detailed instructions.

On another occasion, we received a complaint that the screws holding the windscreen to the body were not being tightened sufficiently. I took this up with Syd and Reg Jackson, the production department's chief inspector, and this produced an unusual reaction. After the assembly team had been told to tighten the screws properly, Syd was given a number of broken bolts with a comment from the line that if the screws had to be tight they would have to be increased in size–despite the fact that many thousand screws had been fitted and properly tightened before. This was an example of the bolshie attitude that was then creeping into the industry and was beginning to show even at MG. In the end, reason prevailed and we had the standard size tightened properly.

Abingdon was also the home of BMC's Competitions Department. Although located actually within the MG factory, this department was directly responsible to BMC. MG provided the services, accommodation and routine administration, but the Competitions Department were always at great pains to make it clear that their corporate loyalty lay with the group as a whole and that the MG marque did not receive any preferential treatment. Understandably, this sometimes led to a certain amount of friction between them and the MG people. The competitions mechanics were a dedicated bunch, with men such as Dougie Watts, Denny Greene, Tommy Wellman, Nobby Clarke, Gerald Whiffen and many others. The head of department was initially wily old Marcus Chambers, who was succeeded by the legendary Stuart Turner. He then handed over to Peter Browning, who was unfortunate to be in charge when the BMC-Leyland merger took place in 1968.

The formation of the British Leyland Motor Corporation was to have far-reaching consequences for Abingdon. MG were to lose many of their design staff and consequently much of their identity, eventually producing only the B and Midget models. The BMC Competitions Department was also cut back drastically: poor Peter Browning lost many of his staff and had to cancel a large part of his forward racing programme. More enlightened management has since recognized the true value of loyalty to a name.

As is often the case, the period preceding the merger saw a great deal of skirmishing behind the scenes, while rumour and counter rumour circulated wildly. The decline of BMC, which made it possible, had really started with the move of their truck operation to Scotland – a development forced upon them by the Government which over-rode their original intention to acquire more factory space at existing sites in the Midlands. As a consequence, truck power units which had previously been made in Coventry and Birmingham with zero service problems now left the Scottish plant in low numbers and gave rise to all sorts of problems. BMC diverted more and more skilled and competent managers north, an an attempt to right the position, but the Scottish factories continued to drain the profits made by the motor car side of the business.

BMC then combined with Jaguar and Pressed Steel to form British Motor Holdings, adding Jaguar and Daimler to their car range, which already included Austin, Morris, Riley, Wolseley, MG and Austin Healey. Daimler and Guy buses and trucks now supplemented the BMC trucks and Nuffield tractors, while Coventry Climax contributed their fork lift trucks, fire pumps and race winning engines. Given time, this giant would surely have risen to the top of the European market, but money was short and profits low, and the company was subject to constant interference.

At this time, Donald Stokes of Leyland started to make his move. Leyland, an old established manufacturer of trucks and buses, had already swallowed Triumph, Rover and Alvis to become a sizeable motor car manufacturer. In addition, Keith Hopkins was organizing a splendid public relations campaign for Leyland that contrasted strongly with BMC's performance in this field. BMC took action to rectify this by bringing in Raymond Baxter as director of motoring publicity. Raymond, an ex-RAF Spitfire pilot and radio and TV broadcaster, did an excellent job, but it was really too late.

Leyland had by now received the backing of the Labour Government, in particular that of Harold Wilson and Anthony Wedgewood-Benn who wanted one big integrated British manufacturer to keep Britain's share of world markets. Meanwhile, Joe Edwards, the managing director of Pressed Steel, was brought back to Longbridge as managing director of BMH, in an attempt to cure the group's troubles. A top motor man, Joe Edwards had been with the industry since he joined Austin in 1928. In my opinion, he might well have saved the day for BMH – but again it was too late. George Harriman, BMH's chairman, was by now a sick man and was in fact rushed to hospital with high blood pressure during a critical stage of the negotiations.

The result of all this activity is now history. The British Leyland Motor Corporation was formed with Donald Stokes as managing director, while both Joe Edwards and George Harriman resigned. The new giant coporation was to suffer the departure of more first class men, such as Bernard Jackman and Lofty England, which inevitably contributed to its sorry performance in subsequent years.

Early on, DMH and I had been faced with a difficult decision, whether to back BMH or throw in our hand with Leyland. Although we were told in plain terms that our future would be brighter with Leyland, all our friends were in BMH and at that time we could not conceive that the smaller company would become the dominant partner. DMH and I discussed the matter at great length and we agreed that our loyalties lay with BMH.

The Competitions Department under Peter Browning had embarked on an ambitious racing programme for 1968, which included support for our Sprites at the Monza 1000 km, the Targa Florio, the Nürburgring 1000 km, the Le Mans 24 hours, and the Rheims 12 hours. This was cut short by the impending merger. In August 1967, Peter wrote me a letter in which he said that he had been asked through John Thornley to pass on Donald Stokes's instructions that they were to make no financial contribution to our racing programme for 1968/9. Peter said that he was not sure whether this instruction covered the motor sporting calendar year or the financial year. Despite this, we continued with the 1968 Le Mans. It was at the unwinding party held after this race that Peter made his odd speech, to the effect that this marked the end of our co-operation – a fact that was by now pretty obvious to all concerned.

Our consulting agreement with BMH still had some time to run but it soon became clear to us that when this ended we would be out in the cold. We therefore decided to channel part of our energies into making a new car. I laid out a design with Barry Bilbie using Vauxhall components. Then Kjell Qvale somehow got to hear about it. He and DMH got together and Kjell decided that he would both market and produce the new car, buying the ailing Jensen Company for this purpose.

The 2.3 litre Vauxhall engine suffered badly when it was modified to meet the US emission regulations which would be in force when the car reached production. Our first choice for an alternative engine was the 3 litre V6 Ford unit, whose characteristics were quite similar to those of the old 3000 unit. Jensen took over the negotiations with Ford for production supplies but failed to reach an agreement. They then decided to go for the new Lotus 16 valve 2 litre engine, which was light, powerful, and very new. We had nothing to do with this decision, all the arrangements being made by Kjell Qvale and Jensen's director of engineering, Kevin Beattie. All these changes of power unit delayed the introduction of the new car, which was finally revealed to the world at the 1972 Geneva Motor Show. Production was scheduled for 200 units a week, a figure Jensen had never achieved with the Big Healey, even when they had all the help from BMC with tooling and supplies. The car was also grossly underpriced: I remember Howard Panton, Jensen's chief engineer, telling me this before the car was introduced, while knowledgeable Ted Eves,

In 1969 freelance stylist Hugo Poole produced this as a design for our new car using Vauxhall units. This later became the Jensen Healey.

John Healey, European Class 2 champion in 1974 and 1977, at speed in his sand yacht. His son, David, has started producing a very fast Class 4 Healey sand yacht, the Sprite of the sand yacht world. (Newswest/International)

of *Autocar*, considered that the poor performance of the British motor industry as a whole could be attributed in part to this type of pricing policy.

Quite naturally, British Leyland did not take kindly to our selling Jensen Healeys side by side with their products from our Warwick showrooms. We thus reluctantly dropped the BL franchise and instead took on a foreign model, FIAT, with which these restrictions did not apply. Whereas our sales department had always considered warranty problems to be too high with BMC cars, these proved negligible when compared to those of the imported cars Geoff Price had to keep running.

My brother Brian was now in poor health and wanted to take up a less frustrating occupation in the milder Cornish climate, while I had little interest in the retail side of the business. Selling Austin Healeys to appreciative, knowledgeable enthusiasts was one thing, but selling transportation to the masses held little appeal for me. We originally intended to sell the property to a developer, who was to incorporate a small engineering workshop and a service shop as part of his development, but this was scotched when the Government introduced restrictions on development. In 1974 we finally sold the company to the Hamblin Group, while retaining complete control of

Healey Automobile Consultants, the engineering interests and the use of the Healey name for cars.

We have since looked at many ways of producing another Healey car, but while the demand increases all the time, the difficulties seem insurmountable. A general lack of confidence in the motor industry's ability to make profits deters the financial investors, while the present-day costs of building a sportscar to meet emission controls on engines and safety legislation are quite simply astronomical. The very high price obtained for Big Healeys today merely reflects in part what a car of this type would cost to put into production. One erroneous report stated that we were working with Honda on a sports car design. I cannot think of any circumstances under which we would work with a Japanese company—they may need help, but we are not about to provide it!

Many people have assumed that DMH and his family accumulated a fortune from a lifetime in the industry. While it is true that a vast fortune passed through our hands, it was all ploughed back into design, research and development, with no thought for the rainy days to come. Nearly all the consultant's fees earned by DMH on vehicles produced by BMC were consumed by these activities. People who sell cars may make a fortune, but the people who build them generally make very little.

Appendices

Original Equipment Suppliers

Lucas Service (with depots in many countries): *all electrical equipment and Girling brakes.*
Smiths Industries Ltd: *all instruments.*
Champion Sparking Plug Co: *sparking plugs.*
Automotive Products Ltd: *Lockheed brakes and Borg & Beck clutches.*
WB Bumpers Ltd (Wilmot Breeden Group), PO Box 204, Almington Rd, Birmingham B25 8EZ, UK. Telephone: 021–706 3344: *bumpers–also re-chrome of bumpers.*
Armstrong Patents Co Ltd, Gibson Lane, Melton, North Ferriby, North Humberside HU14 3HY, UK: *shock absorbers.*
Mintex: *brake pads, linings and clutch facings.*
Associated Engineering: *pistons and bearings.*
GKN: *overdrives, Vandervell bearings, propeller shafts, nuts and bolts.*
Dunlop: *wheels and tyres.*

Do not forget that British Leyland have a world-wide parts and service network. Old established dealers and distributors often have parts for the older models.

All the clubs run spares registers and can offer expert advice on where to get spares and who does the best restoration work. You do not get this sort of help with your modern tin box!

Source of Parts for Austin Healey Sprites and MG Midgets

AH Spares, 427 Tachbrook Road, Whitnash, Leamington Spa, Warwickshire, UK. Telephone: (0926) 20477. (Long-service Healey man with good stocks of parts.)

Moss Motors Ltd, PO Box MG, 5775 Dawson Avenue, Goleta, California, USA. Telephone: (805) 964–6969.

FASPEC, 606 SE Madison, Portland, Oregon, 97214, USA. Telephone: (503) 236–6800.

Southern Carburettors, 49 The Broadway, Wimbledon, London SW19, UK. Telephone: 01–540–8128.

D. J. Sports Cars Ltd, Swains Factory, Crane Mead, Ware, Hertfordshire, UK. Telephone: Ware 66181.

Sports Car Spares, 3510 Cedar Avenue South, Minneapolis, MN 55407, USA. Telephone: (612) 721–3321.

Sports and Classics, 512 Boston Post Road, Darien, CT 06820, USA. Telephone (0223) 832575.

Aleybars, London Road, Sawston, Cambridge CB2 4EF, UK. Telephone: (0223) 832575. (For roll-over bars.)

Mill Accessory Group Ltd, Two Counties Mill, Eaton Bray, Nr. Dunstable, Bedfordshire LU6 2JH, UK. Telephone: (0525) 220671. (Paddy Hopkirk's company supplies some useful sports car equipment.)

Tech Del Ltd, 32–36 Telford Way, Brunel Road, Acton, London W3 7XD, UK. Telephone: 01–743–0103. (Manufacturers of Minilite wheels.)

Restoration Work

Everick Panels, 4a Wise Terrace, Leamington Spa, Warwickshire, UK. Telephone: (0926) 25038. (An old Healey man.)

Walsh Motor Works, 651 E Arques, Sunnyvale, Ca 94086, USA. Telephone: (408) 245–8502.

Don Mollet, PO Box 6542, Santa Barbara, Ca 92111, USA. Telephone: (805) 964–7354.

Jensen Parts and Service Ltd, Kelvin Way, West Bromwich, West Midlands, UK. Telephone: (021) 553 6741.

John Chatham Cars, 138 Gloucester Road, Bishopston, Bristol BS7 8NT, UK. Telephone: (0272) 44154 (Also specializes in tuning Big Healeys for competition.)

Huffaker Engineering, 1290 Holm Road, Petaluma, Ca 94952, USA.

John Britten Garages, Barnet Road, Arkley, Herefordshire, UK. (If you tire of the Spridgets' appearance, John Britten supplies the Arkley kit.)

County Garage, Coventry Road, Warwick, UK. Telephone: (0926) 4401. (If you want to avoid the work of restoring a classic, Roy Standley's garage specializes in good examples.)

Healey West, 130 Shipley Street, San Francisco, Ca 94107. Telephone: (415) 543–4723. (Custom engine rebuilding.)

Recommended Good Reading

Thoroughbred and Classic Cars
Motorsport
Autosport
Motor
Road & Track
Autocar (also have reprint service for road test reports)

Production Figures for Austin Healey Sprites and MG Midgets

	Austin Healey Sprite	MG Midget
1958	8,729	
1959	21,566	
1960	18,665	
1961	10,059	7,656
1962	12,041	9,906
1963	8,852	7,625
1964	11,157	11,450
1965	8,882	9,162
1966	7,024	6,842
1967	6,895	7,854
1968	7,049	7,372
1969	6,133	13,085
1970	1,280	14,811
1971	1,022	16,401
1972		16,243
1973		13,988
1974		11,692
1975		14,478
1976		16,879
1977		14,329
Total:	129,354	199,773

Total production 1958–77: 329,127

Specifications of Austin Healey Sprites and MG Midgets

Model	Sprite	MkII MG Midget		MkII MkIII	MkIII MkIV	MkIII (1500)
Type No. Sprite Midget	HAN5	HAN6 GAN1	HAN7 GAN2	HAN8 GAN3	HAN9 GAN4	
Production dates	1958–61	1961–62	1962–64	1964–66	1966–74	1975 on
Compression ratio	8.3 to 1	9 to 1	8.9 to 1	8.9 to 1	8.8 to 1	9 to 1
bhp at rpm	42.5 at 5000	46 at 5500	56 at 5500	59 at 5750	65 at 6000	65 at 5500
bmep lb/in²	137	138	138	140	143	138
Approx weight lbs	1390	1450	1460	1490	1510	1707
Acceleration (secs)						
0–30 mph	5.2	5.4	4.7	4.3	4.2	4.2
0–50 mph	13.7	13.4	11.5	9.8	7.8	7.8
0–60 mph	20.6	19.3	16.8	14.6	12.3	12.3
0–70 mph	33.6	30.8	26.2	20.4	18.0	18.0
0–80 mph		58.5	38.0	33.4	26.0	25.6
Standing ¼ mile	21.6	21.4	21.0	19.6	18.8	18.8
Max speed – mph	83.5	86.0	88.0	91.0	96.0	101
Typical consumption–mpg	43	40	38	35	33	32

Model	Sprite	MkII MG Midget	MkIII	MkII	MkIV MkIII	MkIII (1500)
Cubic capacity (cc)	948	948	1098	1098	1275	1493
Bore (mm)	62.94	62.94	64.58	64.58	70.61	73.7
Stroke (mm)	76.2	76.2	83.72	83.72	81.28	87.5
Inlet valve dia	1.0937	1.153	1.215	1.215	1.310	1.377
Inlet opens °btdc	5	5	5	5	5	18
Inlet closes °abdc	40	51	51	51	51	58
Exhaust valve dia	1.00	1.00	1.00	1.00	1,154	1.154
Exhaust opens °bbdc	40	51	51	51	51	51
Exhaust closes °atdc	10	21	21	21	21	18
Valve lift	0.280	0.285	0.312	0.312	0.318	
Carburettors	2 × SU H1 1¼ inch	2 × SU HS2 1¼ inch				2 × SU HS4 1½ inch
Carburettor needle	GG	V3	GY	AN	AN	ABT
Spark plug (original)*	N5	N5	N5	N5	N9Y	N9Y
Initial static setting °btdc	5	4	5	5	7	10 at 680 rpm

Recommended tyres Dunlop 5.20 × 13 or Dunlop 145 SR 13

*Note: Champion N9Y is suitable for all unmodified Sprites and Midgets.

Summary of Road Test Figures Taken at the MIRA Test Ground, August 1967

See page 78. The three road tests on the MG Midget followed the standard test procedure laid down for MIRA. The maximum speed is timed over three marked $\frac{1}{4}$-mile sections of the track and the average is recorded. The acceleration figures represent the average of four runs in each direction on the timing straight. These tests were timed on a Swiss Huer marking stop watch which can record the complete sequence of times over one run. The steady speed fuel consumption figures were recorded with the aid of an MGA petrometer.

The figures for the Honda S800 were published by *Motor*, whose road test procedure is very similar to that used at MIRA.

	MG MIDGET AMO 781B Production engine	Engine to 'S' specification	Engine proposed by Morris Engines	Honda S800 (*Motor* 5.8.67)
Axle Ratio	4.22 to 1	3.9 to 1	3.9 to 1	
Maximum speed (mean of 3 quarters) (mph)	96	102	107	97
Lap speed banked track (mph)	95	99	103	94.3
Fuel consumption at steady speed (mpg)				
90	19.0	20.5	23.3	20.0
80	27.3	27.3	30.5	25.0
70	29.0	34.0	34.5	32.0
60	37.7	37.0	42.4	34.0
50	40.7	41.6	41.8	36.0
40	46.5	44.4	46.5	42.0
30	46.5	46.5	50.0	45.0

Top gear acceleration (in seconds)				
10–30	9.4	9.97	9.95	
20–40	9.15	9.35	8.75	19.5
30–50	9.3	8.45	8.1	13.3
40–60	9.5	8.75	7.95	12.7
50–70	10.7	10.0	9.0	14.3
60–80	15.5	13.37	11.4	19.4
Acceleration through gears changing up at 6300 rpm (in seconds)				
0–30	4.0	3.62	3.5	4.2
0–40	6.9	6.32	5.4	6.5
0–50	10.15	9.7	7.95	9.4
0–60	14.2	13.17	11.7	13.6
0–70	20.27	19.10	15.9	18.7
0–80	30.15	28.15	22.9	28.5
Standing $\frac{1}{4}$ mile (in seconds)	19.1	18.8	18.0	19.2

Index